CARLO SCARPA

CARLO SCARPA

Das Handwerk der Architektur
The Craft of Architecture

Herausgegeben von Edited by
Peter Noever

Mit Beiträgen von With contributions by
Tadao Ando, Roberto Gottardi, Arata Isozaki

und einem Gespräch mit and a conversation with
Giovanni Anfodillo

MAK hatje cantz

MAK Studies 3

Diese Publikation erschien anlässlich der Ausstellung
CARLO SCARPA. DAS HANDWERK DER ARCHITEKTUR
MAK Wien, 9. April – 23. November 2003

This book was published on the occasion of the exhibition
CARLO SCARPA. THE CRAFT OF ARCHITECTURE
MAK Vienna, April 9 – November 23, 2003

Ausstellung Exhibition: Peter Noever

Kurator Curator: Rainald Franz

Besonderer Dank Special thanks: Saverio Anfodillo

MAK
Stubenring 5, A-1010 Wien
Tel.: (+43-1) 711 36-0
Fax: (+43-1) 713 10 26
E-Mail: office@MAK.at
www.MAK.at

MAK Center for Art and Architecture, Los Angeles
Schindler House
835 North Kings Road
West Hollywood, CA 90069, USA
Tel.: (+1-323) 651 1510
Fax: (+1-323) 651 2340
E-Mail: office@MAKcenter.org
www.MAKcenter.org

Herausgeber Editor: Peter Noever

Katalogredaktion Catalogue editing: Rainald Franz
Lektorat Copy editing: Sonja Illa-Paschen

Übersetzung Translation: Wolfgang Astelbauer (Deutsch/Englisch
German/English, S. pp. 18, 19, 39, 69–71, 96–121), Karin Fleischanderl
(Italienisch/Deutsch Italian/German, S. pp. 16, 17, 38, 66–68, 90–95),
Michael Strand (Deutsch/Englisch German/English, S. pp. 10–12)
Grafik-Design Graphic design: Maria-Anna Friedl
Herstellung Production: Holzhausen Druck & Medien GmbH

© Texte bei den Autoren Essays by the authors
© Fotos Photos: Georg Mayer/MAK, Peter Kainz/MAK, Fritz Simak/MAK,
Archiv Saverio Anfodillo/MAK: S. p. 102; Guido Guidi: S. pp. 24, 28, 30, 33,
58, 90, 92, 93, 97, 99; Elio Ciol: S. pp. 26, 34, 40, 54, 79; Franco Fonatti:
S. pp. 58, 60, 61, 86; Paolo Monti: S. pp. 44, 52, 62, 56; Peter Noever:
S. p. 6 (links left), 9, 12; Guido Pietropoli: S. p. 6 (rechts right);
Gerald Zugmann/MAK: S. pp. 13, 14, 72, 82, 123
© 2003 MAK, Wien, und Hatje Cantz Verlag, Ostfildern-Ruit

Erschienen im Published by: Hatje Cantz Verlag
Senefelderstraße 12, 73760 Ostfildern-Ruit, Germany
Tel.: (+49-711) 4 40 50, Fax: (+49-711) 4 40 52 20
www.hatjecantz.com

Hatje Cantz books are available internationally at selected bookstores
and from the following distribution partners:

USA/North America – D.A.P., Distributed Art Publishers, New York,
www.artbook.com
France – Interart, Paris, interart.paris@wanadoo.fr
UK – Art Books International, London, sales@art-bks.com
Belgium – Exhibitions International, Leuven, www.exhibitionsinternational.be
Australia – Towerbooks, French Forest (Sydney), towerbks@zipworld.com.au

For Asia, Japan, South America, and Africa, as well as for general questions,
please contact Hatje Cantz directly at sales@hatjecantz.de, or visit our
homepage www.hatjecantz.com for further information.

ISBN 3-7757-1403-0

Printed in Austria

Inhalt Contents

Peter Noever
Der andere Architekt — 7
The Other Architect — 10

Roberto Gottardi
Testimonio — 16
Testimonio — 18

Villen / Innenraumgestaltungen Villas / Interior Design — 20

Tadao Ando
Die Architektur Carlo Scarpas — 38
The Architecture of Carlo Scarpa — 39

Museen / Ausstellungsgestaltungen Museums / Exhibition Designs — 40

Arata Isozaki
Der letzte Traum — 66
The Last Dream — 69

Tomba Brion — 72

Carlo Scarpa und and Saverio Anfodillo
„WIR WAREN EIN TEAM" — 91
"WE WERE A TEAM" — 96

Biografie Biography — 103

Ausgewählte Projekte Selected Projects — 104

Ausgewählte Bibliografie Selected Bibliography — 107

Zeichnungen, Planpausen und Modelle im Bestand des MAK — 108
Drawings, blueprints, and models owned by the MAK

Carlo Scarpa: „Kann Architektur Poesie sein?", Diavortrag, Akademie der bildenden Künste Wien, 1976
Carlo Scarpa: "Can Architecture be Poetry?", slide lecture, Academy of Fine Arts Vienna, 1976

Der andere Architekt

Das Sublime in der Architektur

Peter Noever

In Vicenza, in den Pferdestallungen der Villa Almerico „La Rotonda", hatte ich eine meiner allererste Begegnungen mit Carlo Scarpa. Die monolithischen Pferdetränken übersät mit Skizzen, Zeichnungen, Arbeitsutensilien erklärte er mit der leisen Ironie und nicht ganz ohne den Stolz des geschichtsbewussten „Meisters aus dem Zeitalter des Humanismus, der zufällig im 20. Jahrhundert lebt", wie er einmal genannt wurde, dies sei der ihm angemessene Ort, denn schließlich sei er kein Palladio.

Scarpa war ein Solitär; in stilistischer Hinsicht ein Einzelgänger nicht nur unter den italienischen Architekten, der den Dialog – mit Künstlern ebenso wie mit seinen Handwerkern – suchte, ohne sich je zu verbünden. Er war davon überzeugt, dass alles im richtigen Augenblick passieren, jeder Handgriff perfekt sein muss, ohne dabei einen Unterschied zwischen der Arbeit und dem alltäglichen Leben anzuerkennen. So konnte er bis spät in die Nacht mit Handwerkern um die Lösung eines Problems ringen, selbst wenn er diese nur mit dem Angebot, sie anschließend selbst nach Hause bringen zu lassen, zu derartigen Sonderschichten bewegen konnte; ebenso kam es vor, dass er mitten während eines Essens, wenn er die venezianische Kultur des Kochens in Gefahr wähnte, in die Küche des Restaurants eindrang, um den verblüfften Köchen und Gästen die Zubereitung einer authentischen Pasta zu demonstrieren.

Außer von Frank Lloyd Wright zeigte er sich in seiner frühen Jugend von der Wiener Secession, vor allem von Olbrich und Hoffmann beeindruckt, ohne dass dies jedoch weitere Kontakte zu dieser Stadt zur Folge gehabt hätte.

Schließlich bestätigte er in einem Brief an die Akademie der bildenden Künste den Termin für seine erste Wiener Ausstellung mit Juni 1975. Am 16. November 1976 hielt er dann ebendort eine Gastvorlesung unter dem Titel „Kann Architektur Poesie sein?" Der temperamentvolle, in seiner Heimat meist respekt- und liebevoll „il professore" genannte Venezianer ließ diesen seinen ersten und einzigen Wiener Auftritt – während dessen er leidenschaftlich zur Architektur Stellung bezog – zu einem besonderen Ereignis werden.

Was der ausgebildete Bildhauer und Architekt „honoris causa" damals zum Vortrag brachte, war ein bedingungsloses Plädoyer für utopische Visionen, für eine Architektur, die ausschließlich Kunst und Kultur verpflichtet ist – auch gegen die Realität, gegen die Mächtigen. Es waren Worte, die aus dem Munde Scarpas, der seine Auffassung, Architektur könne Poesie sein, ebenso humorvoll wie unnachgiebig vorgetragen hatte, authentisch und überzeugend geklungen haben, in derselben Art, wie es ihm gelungen war, sie mit seinem Werk zu realisieren. 72-jährig in voller Lebenskraft und voller Tatendrang, seine verspätete internationale Anerkennung genießend, verstarb Scarpa am 28. November 1978 völlig überraschend in der japanischen Stadt Sendai. Die Umstände dieses Todes muten an wie eine Ironie des Schicksals, starb er doch infolge eines Sturzes über eine Treppe – er, der das Motiv der Treppe in allen seinen Bauwerken immer wieder aufgegriffen hatte.

Die Wiener Ausstellung kam damals nicht zustande, scheiterte an der Stadt, die sich allzu gerne mit dem bereits Anerkannten schmückt. Zu Lebzeiten Carlo Scarpas war es nicht gelungen, seine Arbeit in Wien zu zeigen. Reichlich verspätet, aber mit dem Anliegen und der Kenntnis, der Arbeit und dem Temperament des Architekten gerecht zu werden, zeigte das MAK 1989 dann die Ausstellung „Carlo Scarpa. Die andere Stadt".* Sie beschränkte sich auf ein einziges Projekt, die Grabanlage Brion in San Vito d'Altivole/Treviso. Die großen Ausstellungshallen waren mit einer Unzahl von Zeichentischen bestückt, auf denen unter Glas 1.300 Skizzen und Zeichnungen, somit die gesamte gezeichnete Dokumentation seines vielschichtigsten Projekts, präsentiert wurden. Durch diese Konzentration auf seine Methode und besondere Arbeitsweise dürfte es gelungen sein, in die Sinnes- und Gedankenwelt des Architekten einzudringen – schließlich hatte er stets praktisch alle architektonischen Entscheidungen über den Weg des Zeichnens getroffen – und sie in ihrer Unbeugsamkeit noch einmal in Erinnerung zu rufen.

1999 gelang es dem MAK als sichtbares Zeichen meiner über 30-jährigen Auseinandersetzung mit Scarpa 224 Zeichnungen aus dessen Nachlass zu erstehen, heute die umfassendste Dokumentation seines Werks außerhalb des Besitzes des italienischen Staates, der das Archiv ebenfalls erst in jüngster Zeit erworben hat.

Aus diesem Anlass ergaben sich 2003 die Ausstellung „Carlo Scarpa. Das Handwerk der Architektur" im MAK-Kunstblättersaal sowie die vorliegende Publikation.

Scarpa hatte über vierzig Jahre lang geistvoll, in gewisser Weise aristokratisch, leicht ironisch und gänzlich undidaktisch an der Kunstakademie in Venedig gelehrt und damit den Großteil seines Lebens in dieser Region verbracht. Dennoch musste er, unzweifelhaft einer der bedeutendsten Lehrer der Architektur und ab 1972 Rektor des Instituts für Architektur an der Universität von Venedig, immer um die Realisierung seiner Bauwerke kämpfen, da stets aufs Neue versucht wurde, ihn unter dem Vorwand mangelnder „Befugnis" daran zu hindern.

Er wurde aber nicht nur wegen seiner herausragenden Arbeiten hoch geschätzt, sondern auch als Mensch, der glaubhaft nie Verrat an seinen eigenen Vorstellungen begangen hat. Diese so seltene Übereinstimmung zwischen den Vorstellungen und Ansprüchen und ihren Verwirklichungen ließ die Begegnungen mit seiner Person ebenso zu einem unvergesslichen Ereignis werden wie die Begegnung mit seiner Arbeit, der es immer wieder gelingt, „alte" Wahrheiten in einer modernen Architektursprache zu formulieren.

So erreicht diese stille, eindringliche Architektur die Leichtigkeit sublimer Zwecklosigkeit. Sie eröffnet Erfahrungen des Unvorhergesehenen, Erstaunlichen; es ist die gebaute Erfahrung einer außergewöhnlich modernen Fantasie, die, aus der venezianischen Kulturlandschaft heraustretend, als reine Architektur deren Geschichte erzählt.

Für Scarpa war Architektur Lebensraum, das Leben selbst eine Art Kunstform. Daraus entspringt die sensible Dialogfähigkeit seiner Bauten – sowohl mit der Natur als auch mit der Kultur, in die er sie integriert: Lichtspiele und -reflexe, Geräusche von Wasser, sich einnisterndes Moos … Wie kaum einem anderen Architekten gelingt es ihm, Details zu artikulieren, ohne sich und das Ganze des Entwurfs an sie zu verlieren. Oft wird dies ermöglicht durch die unorthodoxe Verbindung von Materialien auf der Grundlage überlieferten Wissens oder durch die Zusammenführung von Formensprachen unterschiedlichster Herkunft aus dem Okzident und dem gerade Venedig so nahen Orient und die sich dadurch ermöglichende Symbolik. Immer ist es das Überschreiten der Funktion durch den Ausdruck, das seine Arbeiten aus der starren Dingwelt heraustreten lässt und sie dem Leben näher bringt.

Carlo Scarpa trifft Peter Noever und dessen Studenten der Akademie der bildenden Künste Wien zu Dreharbeiten für den Dokumentarfilm „Kann Architektur Poesie sein?" auf dem Gelände der Grabanlage Tomba Brion, San Vito d'Altivole, April 1978

* Ausstellungskomitee: Manlio Brusatin, Venedig; Philippe Duboy, Paris; Peter Noever, Wien; Nini Scarpa, Venedig; Tobia Scarpa, Trevignano; Hiroyuki Toyoda Venedig–Tokio.
Ausstellungsgestaltung: Peter Noever, Hiroyuki Toyoda; Organisation: Johannes Wieninger.

The Other Architect
On the Sublime in Architecture

Peter Noever

It was in Vicenza, in the horse stables of the Villa Almerico "La Rotonda", when I had one of my first encounters with Carlo Scarpa. To account for the monolithic horse troughs scattered with sketches, drawings, working utensils, he said – with quiet irony and not without the pride of an historically aware "master from the age of Humanism who happened to live in the 20th century", as he had been called – that this was an adequate place for him. After all, he added, he was not a Palladio.

Scarpa was a singular personality, stylistically a maverick – not only among Italian architects. He sought dialogue, with other artists as well as with the craftsmen working for him, without ever fraternizing. He was convinced that there was a right moment for everything, that every stroke of work must be perfect, without making a difference between work and everyday life. He was the type of person who would negotiate late into the night with his workmen to get things done the way he wanted them, even if, in order to get them to do these extra shifts, he had to promise to drive them home afterwards. Or he would stomp into a restaurant kitchen, whenever he felt that Venetian cuisine was at stake, to demonstrate to the baffled cooks and guests how an authentic pasta is made.

Aside from Frank Lloyd Wright, he was impressed by the Vienna Secession in his early youth, especially by Olbrich and Hoffmann, though this did not lead to any closer contacts with, or in, this city.

Finally, he confirmed, in a letter written to the Academy of Fine Arts, the dates appointed for his first exhibition in Vienna in June 1975. On November 16, 1976, he gave a lecture at the Academy which was entitled "Can Architecture be Poetry?" The temperamental Venetian – mostly called "il professore" in his hometown with respect and affection – made this first and only public appearance in Vienna a truly special event in which he made a passionate case for architecture.

What the sculptor by training and architect "honoris causa" put forth on the occasion was an uncompromising argument for utopian vision, for a kind of architecture that is committed to art and culture only – even if this should go against reality or against those in power. These were words that sounded authentic and convincing from the mouth of Scarpa who expounded his idea that architecture could be poetry with humor as much as with adamancy quite in the same manner in which he had been able to make it materialize in his work.

72 years old and full of life and activity, enjoying his somewhat belated international recognition, Scarpa died, completely unexpectedly, on November 28, 1978, in the Japanese city of Sendai. The circumstances of his death come as an irony of fate; he who had always liked to use stairs as an architectural motif died from a fall down the stairs.

The Vienna exhibition was eventually cancelled. The project ran aground in this city which prefers to adorn itself with the well-established. In his lifetime, Carlo Scarpa had no chance to present his work here. Rather late, though with a commitment to, and in the knowledge of paying overdue tribute to this architect's work and temperament, the MAK in 1989 showed an exhibition entitled "Carlo Scarpa. The Other City", which confined itself to one specific project, the Brion Tomb in San Vito d'Altivole, Treviso, Italy. The large exhibition rooms were equipped with countless drawing tables showing, under glass, no less than 1,300 sketches and drawings, and hence the entire body of drawings documenting Scarpa's most complex project. The concentration on his approach and working method afforded an insight into the perceptual and intellectual world of this architect, who had arrived at virtually all his architectural decisions by way of drawing, evoking once more their uncompromising austerity.

In 1999, the MAK managed, as a visible manifestation of my thirty-year study of Scarpa's oeuvre, to purchase 224 drawings from his estate, until today the most comprehensive documentation of his work outside the holdings of the Republic of Italy which also acquired the archives only recently.

This occasion prompted the 2003 exhibition "Carlo Scarpa. The Craft of Architecture" at the MAK Works on Paper Room as well as this publication.

For more than forty years, Scarpa was a teacher – brilliant, in a way aristocratic, slightly ironic and entirely undidactic – at the Venice Academy of Art, spending the most part of his life in this region. Nevertheless, he – without doubt the most eminent teacher of architecture and, from 1972, director of the Academy Department of Architecture – always had to struggle in order to realize his projects as there were recurrent attempts to inhibit him on grounds of an alleged lack of "professional qualification."

He was appreciated not only for his work, but also as a person who never betrayed his own ideas. This rare congruence between ideas and self-chosen standards and their materialization made encounters with him an unforgettable experience. Encounters with his work always succeeded in formulating again "old" truths in a modern architectural language.

Thus this quiet and impressive architecture attains the lightness of sublime freedom of purpose, enabling an experience of the unpredictable, of the amazing; it is the built experience of an exceptional modern imagination which, emerging from the Venetian cultural landscape, recounts architectural history in terms of architecture itself.

For Scarpa, architecture was living space and life was itself a kind of art. This is where the sensitive, dialogical quality of his buildings comes from – a dialogue both with nature and with the culture in which he integrates them. The play, the reflexes of light, sounds of water, gathering moss … Like hardly any other architect, he is able to articulate details without getting lost in them, without losing himself and the general outline of the design. In many cases, this is made possible through an unorthodox combination of materials on the basis of knowledge passed down by tradition, or through the merging of formal languages of widely different origins, from the Occident or the Orient, with its particular affinity to Venice, and the symbolism thus engendered. It is always the transcending of function by expression which makes his works emerge from the rigid object world and brings them closer to life.

Carlo Scarpa meets Peter Noever and his students from the Academy of Fine Arts Vienna who have come for the shooting of the documentary "Can Architecture be Poetry?" at the Brion Tomb, San Vito d'Altivole, April 1978

* Exhibition Committee: Manlio Brusatin, Venice; Philippe Duboy, Paris; Peter Noever, Vienna; Nini Scarpa, Venice; Tobia Scarpa, Trevignano; Hiroyuki Toyoda, Venice and Tokyo.
Exhibition Design: Peter Noever, Hiroyuki Toyoda; Project Management: Johannes Wieninger.

Ausstellung „Carlo Scarpa. Die andere Stadt"
Exhibition "Carlo Scarpa. The Other City"
MAK-Ausstellungshalle Exhibition Hall, 1989/90

Ausstellung „Carlo Scarpa. Die andere Stadt"
Exhibition "Carlo Scarpa. The Other City"
MAK-Ausstellungshalle Exhibition Hall, 1989/90

Ausstellung „Carlo Scarpa. Das Handwerk der Architektur"
Exhibition "Carlo Scarpa. The Draft of Architecture"
MAK-Kunstblättersaal Works on Paper Room, 2003

Testimonio

Roberto Gottardi

Ich glaube Carlo Scarpa war die Person, die meine Entwicklung als Architekt am stärksten beeinflusst hat.

Seine Kritik ging immer weit über einzelne Projekte hinaus, sie bezog das Alltägliche, die unbedeutendsten Dinge mit ein: als zum Beispiel der Kugelschreiber aufkam, den er im Vergleich zur Füllfeder für unpersönlich hielt und für ungeeignet, Stimmungen und Gefühlszustände wiederzugeben, oder der Minenstift, der seine Funktion zwar perfekt erfüllt, jedoch des Zaubers, der einem normalen Bleistift innewohnt, völlig entbehrt. Und das nicht aus einer absurden Nostalgie heraus oder weil er dem Neuen gegenüber nicht offen gewesen wäre, sondern weil er den Phänomenen des Alltags kritisch gegenüberstand, wobei es ihm immer um das Wesentliche ging. Es lag ihm völlig fern, etwas zu akzeptieren, nur weil es nahe liegend war oder weil alle anderen es akzeptierten.

Durch dieses ständige Infragestellen, durch das Miteinbeziehen aller Lebenserfahrungen war er ein höchst sensibler Architekt, und jede Begegnung mit ihm war eine Bereicherung. Nach einer solchen Begegnung kehrte ich stets voller Enthusiasmus und mit geschärfter Wahrnehmung allen Aspekten des Lebens gegenüber zu meinen eigenen Projekten zurück.

Er nahm sich viel Zeit für Kritik, er empfing mich sogar bei sich zu Hause, zweifellos eine schmeichelhafte Tatsache, denn er stellte hohe Ansprüche und war in dieser Hinsicht sehr streng.

Scarpa als „Architekt des Details" zu bezeichnen, wie manche Kritiker es getan haben, ist gewiss ungerecht und einengend. All jene, die versuchen, ihn nur in diesem Punkt zu imitieren, oder die glauben, die Liebe zum Detail sei alles, was man von ihm lernen könne, waren von Anfang an zum Scheitern verurteilt – aber leider gibt es jede Menge ausschließlich unter diesem Aspekt agierende „Scarpianer".

Ich habe nicht nur durch seine Kritik gelernt, sondern gleichzeitig auch durch seine Werke, von denen viele leider zerstört oder im Laufe der Zeit verändert worden sind.

Wenn er ein neues Projekt in Angriff nahm, war das immer sehr aufregend und immer etwas Neues, Neuartiges, er wiederholte sich nie.

In der Zeit, in der ich an der Universität studierte, machten ihm zahlreiche Missverständnisse das Leben schwer. Gewisse Leute wollten ihn sogar an der Ausübung seiner Tätigkeit hindern, weil er keinen Titel als Architekt hatte, während doch seine Werke unter Beweis stellten, dass er in Venedig der beste war. Wiederum andere verweigerten ihm die amtliche Anerkennung seiner Projekte, etwa der Renovierung der Galleria Querini Stampalia im Jahr 1973, obwohl er aufgrund seiner Verdienste im Jahr zuvor zum Rektor des Istituto Universitario di Architettura in Venedig ernannt worden war.

Später erhielt er jedoch zahlreiche Anerkennungen, und ich freute mich sehr, dass sein Werk in so vielen Ländern verbreitet und sehr geschätzt wurde.

Vorbildhaft war er auch in seiner Fähigkeit, sich respektvoll und dennoch glaubwürdig dem venezianischen Ambiente anzuverwandeln. Während immer mehr verlogen anonyme, ethisch verurteilungswürdige Gebäude entstanden, die sich dem Problem nicht einmal stellten, offenbarte sich seine „Venezianitá" unter anderem – wie am Beispiel der Galleria Querini deutlich zu sehen – in Lichtspielen, in den vielfach gebrochenen Reflexen des Wassers, aber nie als mimetische Architektur, auch wenn er Anleihen bei tradierten Formen nahm.

Was ich bei Scarpa gelernt hatte, kam mir vor allem zugute, als ich in einem anderen Land, unter völlig anderen Bedingungen arbeitete. Es half mir, die richtige Antwort auf gewiss nicht einfache und komplexe Bedingungen wie etwa in Kuba zu finden, einem Land, das auf der Suche nach Autonomie und kultureller Identität ist.

Ich bin dem MAK sehr dankbar, mich zu diesem Statement aufgefordert zu haben, das keinen Anspruch auf vollständige, kritische Darstellung erhebt. Und vor allem dafür, dass es wieder einmal eine Initiative ins Leben gerufen hat, die einem der bedeutendsten Vertreter der zeitgenössischen Architektur Gerechtigkeit widerfahren lässt.

Testimonio

Roberto Gottardi

Carlo Scarpa was the person that probably had the most decisive influence on my development as an architect.
His criticism was not limited to individual projects but included the ordinary, the most insignificant things. For example, he was critical of the emergence of the ballpoint pen, which he regarded as impersonal compared to the fountain pen, and unsuitable for describing moods or emotional states: and he was critical of the lead pen, which, despite its perfect functionalism, completely lacked the charm of a conventional pen. His attitude did not spring from any absurd nostalgia or a rejection of new things but from a critical attitude towards everyday phenomena and an uncompromising interest in the essential. Nothing was further from his mind than accepting something because it was obvious or accepted by everybody.
This persistent questioning and the inclusion of all experiences of life made him a highly sensitive architect, and I have gained a lot from each encounter with him. After meeting him, I always returned to my projects full of enthusiasm and with a sharpened perception regarding all facets of life.
He really took his time when criticizing my approaches and even invited me to visit him at home, which flattered me because he was very strict with all people that did not meet his expectations.
Calling Scarpa "an architect of details," as some critics did, is definitely unjust and beside the point. Those who try to imitate this dimension of his understanding of architecture or believe that his love of details is everything to be learned from him were doomed to fail from the very beginning. Unfortunately, there are quite a lot of "followers" who see themselves only under this aspect.
I have learned a lot both from Scarpa's critical remarks and his works, many of which have regrettably been destroyed or modified in the course of time. It was also very exciting for me when he started working on a new project because he never repeated himself. When I was studying at the university, numerous misunderstandings made life difficult for him. Certain people even tried to prevent him from practicing his profession since he did not have the title of Architect, even though his works evidenced that he was the best in Venice. Others refused to formally approve of projects such as the renovation of the Galleria Querini Stampalia in 1973, despite the fact that Scarpa had been appointed Head of the Istituto Universitario di Architettura in Venice on account of his merits the year before.

Later, he won recognition from many sides, and I was very glad that his œuvre became known and highly acclaimed in numerous countries.

His ability to make the Venetian ambience his own in an equally respectful and plausible way, also contributed to making him an example for me. While an increasing number of mendaciously anonymous, ethically reprehensible buildings mushroomed, his *venezianità* clearly revealed itself – as the Galleria Querini exemplifies – in his play with light, in the manifold refractions of water, but never in mimetic architectural designs, even f he based his projects on tradition.

What I learned from Scarpa benefited me especially when I began to work in another country under completely different circumstances. He helped me to find the right answer to conditions that were anything but simple, in a country like Cuba that was searching for its autonomy and cultural identity.

I am very grateful to the MAK for asking me to make this statement which, of course, is not aimed at being a comprehensive critical evaluation. And I am happy that the MAK has again started an initiative that does justice to one of the most important representatives of contemporary architecture.

Villen / Innenraumgestaltungen
Villas / Interior Design

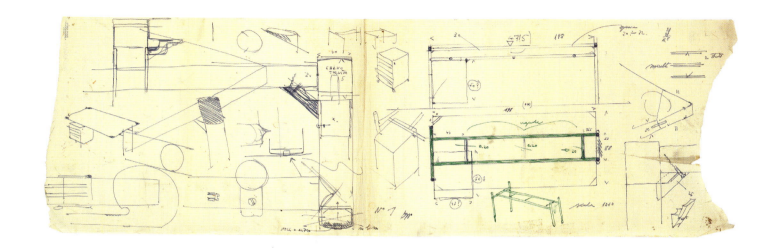

Schreibmöbel für Nini Scarpa
Entwurfszeichnung mit Details und Querschnitten
der Trägerkonstruktion mit Angaben des Materials
und der Maße
o. J.
Entwurfspapier, blauer, grüner Filzstift

Desk for Nini Scarpa
Draft with details and sections of the supporting
construction with specifications concerning the
material and measurements
Undated
Sketching paper, blue, green felt tip

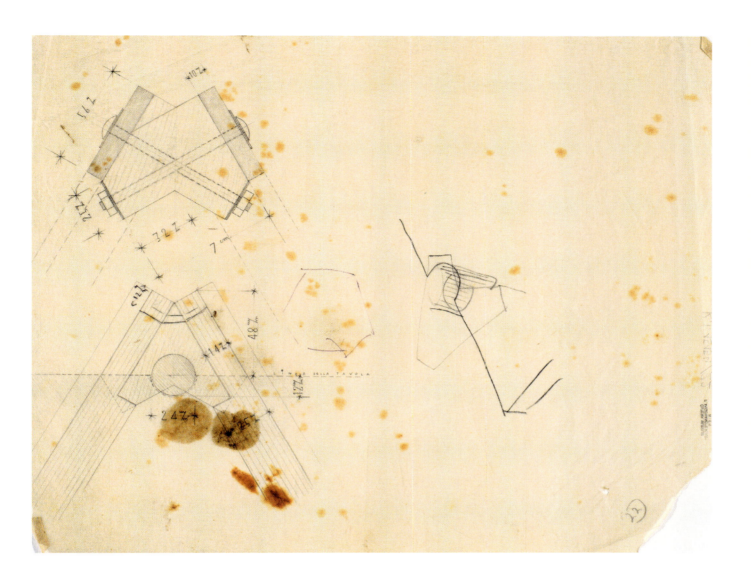

Tisch für Luigi Nono
Details der Winkel und der Verschraubung
o. J.
Entwurfspapier, Bleistift

Table for Luigi Nono
Details of angles and screws
Undated
Sketching paper, pencil

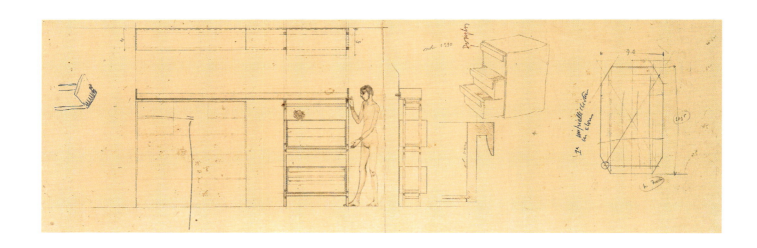

Bibliothek mit Porträt von Tobia Scarpa
Doppelseitiger Entwurf für Bücherregale und Ladenelemente mit Angabe des Materials, Zeichnung von Tobia Scarpa als „Modulor"
o. J.
Entwurfskarton, Bleistift, Kugelschreiber

Library with portrait of Tobia Scarpa
Designs of shelves and drawers with material specifications on recto and verso, portrait of Tobia Scarpa as "modulor"
Undated
Cardboard, pencil, ballpoint

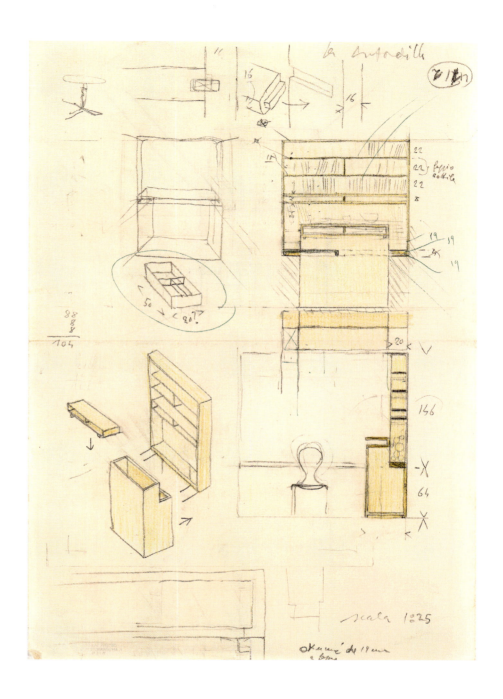

Bücherregal für die Schwägerin Carlo Scarpas
Perspektive und Front mit Detailskizzen und Materialangaben
o. J.
Karton, Bleistift, Tinte, roter Buntstift

Bookshelf for Carlo Scarpa's sister-in-law
Perspective and front with detail sketches
and material specifications
Undated
Cardboard, pencil, ink, red crayon

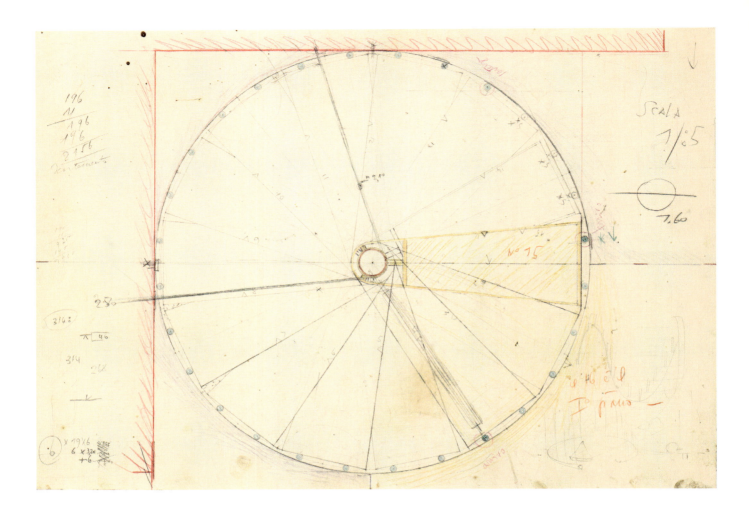

Wendeltreppe für das Haus Muraro, Venedig
Aufsicht der Spindel mit Angaben zu den Maßen,
Maßstab 1:5, doppelseitig bezeichnet
1975
Entwurfskarton, Bleistift, roter, blauer, gelber,
orange Buntstift, verso nur Bleistift

Spiral staircase for the Muraro House, Venice
Top view of newel with details concerning
measurements, scale 1:5, drawings on recto and verso
1975
Cardboard, pencil, red, blue, yellow, orange
crayon, only pencil on verso

Wendeltreppe für das Haus Muraro, Venedig
Aufsicht des Ständers und der ansetzenden
Stufe mit Details der Konstruktion, Maßen und
Materialangaben
1975
Planpause mit Korrekturen in Bleistift, gelbem
Buntstift

Spiral staircase for the Muraro House, Venice
Top view of post and first step with construction
details, measurements, and material specifications
1975
Blueprint with pencil and yellow crayon revisions

Villen / Innenraumgestaltungen 24

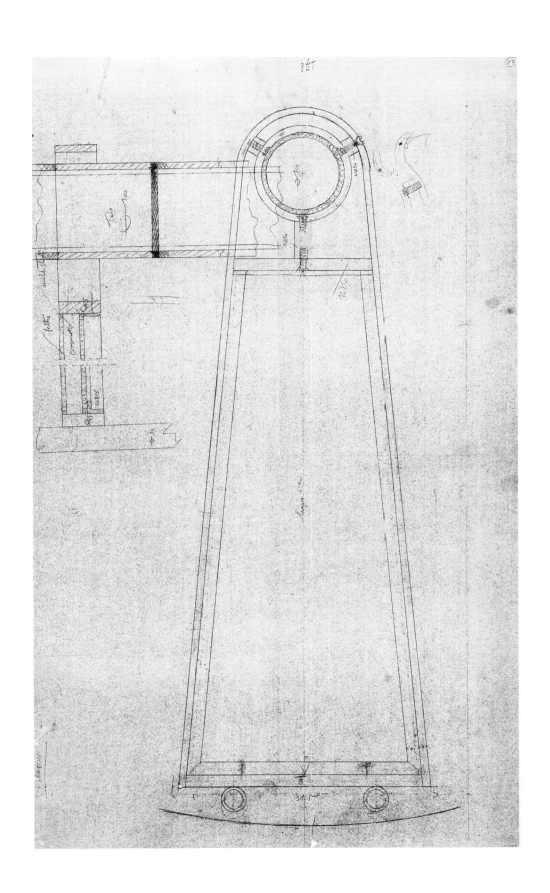

Aula Tribunale (Schwurgerichtssaal)
„Manlio Capitolo", Venedig, 1955
Die paraventartige hölzerne Verkleidung der Wände, die hinsichtlich des Materials ihre Entsprechung in der Möblierung findet, lässt den Gerichtssaal als streng geometrisches Raumkunstwerk erscheinen. Einzig die marmorne Schrifttafel, gerahmt in Silber und Kupfer, bringt die Symmetrie des Raums bewusst aus dem Gleichgewicht.

Aula Tribunale (civil courtroom)
"Manlio Capitolo", Venice, 1955
The wooden, screen-like paneling of the walls, which corresponds to the furniture of the room in its material, makes the civil courtroom appear as an austerely geometric space within a space. Only the silver- and copper-framed marble plate with the inscription is aimed at destroying the symmetric balance of the room.

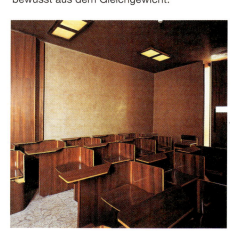

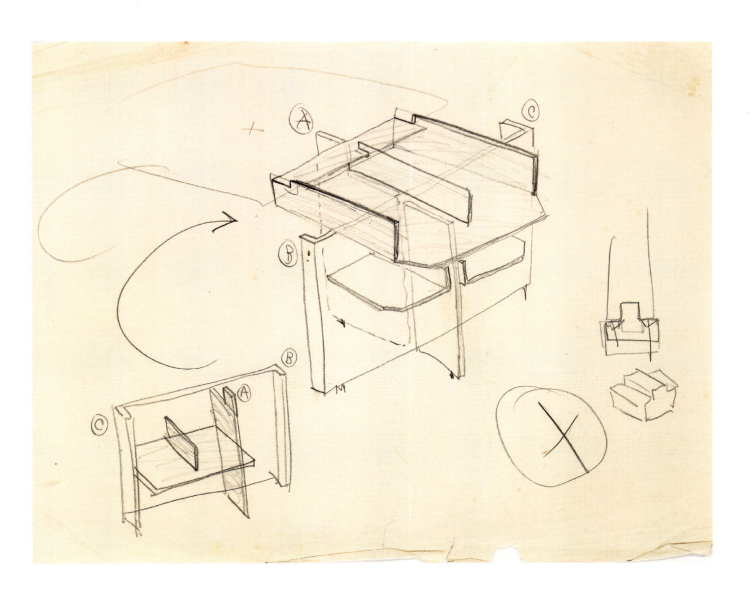

Aula Tribunale „Manlio Capitolo", Venedig
Konstruktionsskizze Carlo Scarpas mit Details
für den Tisch der Richter, doppelseitig
1955
Papier, Bleistift

Aula Tribunale "Manlio Capitolo", Venice
Construction sketch by Carlo Scarpa with details
of the judges' table, recto and verso
1955
Paper, pencil

Haus Zentner, Zürich, 1961–66
Das für die Familie Zentner in Zürich umgestaltete Gebäude ist im Kern eine Villa aus dem Jahr 1914. Scarpa definiert das Sockelgeschoss durch Mauerwerk und Beton, während sich große Glasflächen in den oberen Stockwerken der neu gestalteten Fassaden im Westen, Norden und Osten öffnen. Erstmals sind hier Architekturmotive zur Verhüllung des Bestehenden angelegt, etwa das Bullaugenfenster oder das horizontale Mosaik an der Wohnzimmerdecke, die in späteren Schöpfungen Carlo Scarpas – etwa im Möbelgeschäft Gavina oder in der Tomba Brion – wieder auftauchen. Bei der Innenraumgestaltung setzt Carlo Scarpa starke persönliche Akzente im Sinne der Auftraggeber. Für das Haus Zentner entsteht auch der luxuriöse Esstisch, der unter dem Namen „Doge" 1968 in vereinfachter Form in Produktion geht.

Zentner House, Zurich, 1961–66
The core of the building redesigned for the Zentner family in Zurich is a villa erected in 1914. Scarpa defines the basement floor by means of masonry and concrete, while large glass areas structure the upper floors of the redesigned façades in the west, north, and east. Here, Scarpa uses architectural elements, such as the porthole window or the horizontal mosaic on the dining room ceiling, to hide extant parts for the first time – a measure which recurs in later designs like the furniture shop Gavina or the Tomba Brion. Following his client's wishes, Carlo Scarpa sets a decisively personal tone as regards the interior design. He also creates a luxurious dining room table which goes into production in a simplified form under the name "Doge" in 1968.

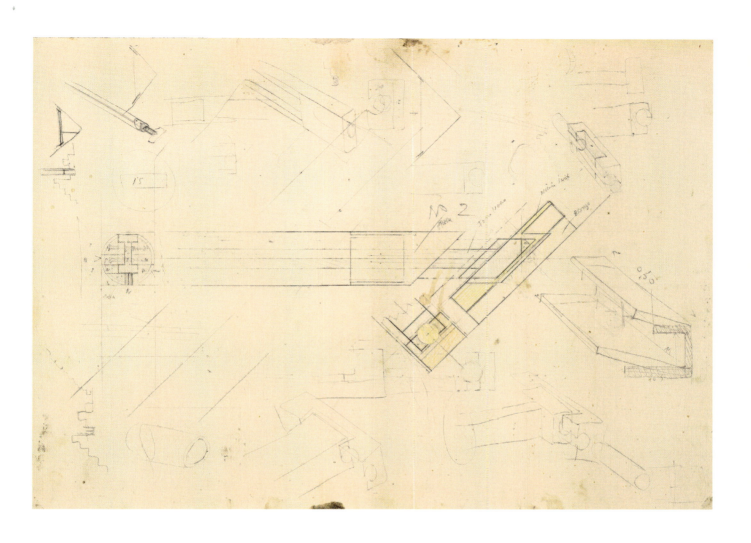

Haus Zentner, Zürich
Querschnitte und Perspektiven der Halterungen
1961–66
Karton, Bleistift, gelber, blauer, orange Buntstift

Zentner House, Zurich
Sections and perspectives of the fixtures
1961–66
Cardboard, pencil, yellow, blue, orange crayon

Tisch „Doge" (1968)
Tisch „Valmarana" (1972)
Tisch „Quatuor" (1972)
Erst 1968 entsteht mit dem Tisch „Doge" das erste Möbel Carlo Scarpas, das serienmäßig und nicht nur für einen einzelnen Auftraggeber gefertigt wird. Bis 1977 schließt sich daran eine Anzahl besonders klar gestalteter Möbel, die heute zu den Klassikern italienischen Designs zählen.

Table „Doge" (1968)
Table „Valmarana" (1972)
Table „Quatuor" (1972)
Carlo Scarpa's first piece of furniture which is not only made for an individual client but also goes into serial manufacture, the table "Doge," dates from as late as 1968. Until 1977, this table was followed by a number of extraordinarily clear-cut pieces which are regarded as classics of Italian design today.

Tisch für das Haus Zentner
Table for the Zentner House

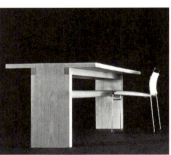

Doge

Valmarana

Quatuor

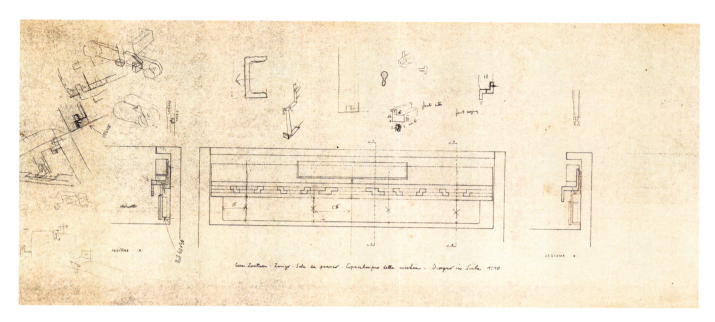

Haus Zentner, Zürich
Heizkörperabdeckung der Nische im
Speisesaal, mit Material- und Maßangaben,
2 Querschnitte
1961–66
Planpause, mit Bleistift überzeichnet

Zentner House, Zurich
Radiator cover for the dining room recess,
with details concerning the material and
measurements, 2 sections
1961–66
Blueprint, pencil revisions

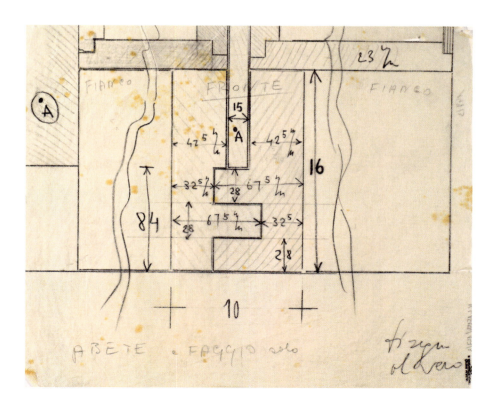

Haus Zentner, Zürich
Detailskizze für den Raumteiler, Querschnitt
mit Maßangaben, Originalmaß, Zeichnung
Carlo Scarpas
1961–66
Velin, Bleistift

Zentner House, Zurich
Sketch of details for partition, cross-section,
original dimensions, drawing by Carlo Scarpa
1961–66
Vellum paper, pencil

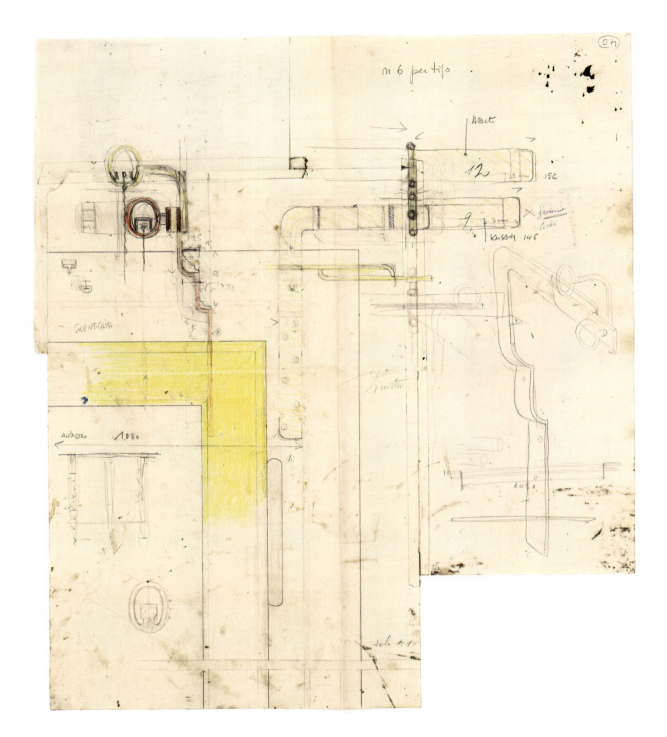

Vorhangstange
Querschnitt und Detailzeichnung in Originalgröße
im Verhältnis zum ebenfalls angelegten
Fensterrahmen
o. J.
2 Kartonteile, Entwurfspapier, mit Klebeband
zusammengefügt, collagiert, Bleistift, gelber,
roter Buntstift

Curtain rod
Cross-section and detail drawing of the rod in its
original dimension in relation to the also depicted
window frame
Undated
2 cardboard parts, sketching paper, joined with
adhesive tape, collaged, pencil, yellow, red crayon

**Aula Magna di Ca' Foscari,
Universität Venedig, 1955/56**
Die Umgestaltung der Aula der Universität Venedig stellt Carlo Scarpas direkteste Auseinandersetzung mit der Stützenarchitektur des von ihm so bewunderten amerikanischen Architekten Frank Lloyd Wright dar. Wieder stellt sich Scarpa die Aufgabe, in der Hülle eines historischen Bauwerks einen zeitgenössischen Ansprüchen und moderner ästhetischer Wahrnehmung genügenden Raum zu entwerfen. Der hölzerne Einbau Scarpas betont das gotische Skelett des Gebäudes.

**Aula Magna di Ca' Foscari,
Venice University, 1955/56**
The redesign of the Venice University auditorium represents Scarpa's most immediate exploration of the post-and-lintel construction so crucial for the work of Frank Lloyd Wright, the American architect he admires so much. Again, Scarpa aimes at creating a room within the shell of the historical building that comes up to modern requirements and aesthetic principles of perception. Scarpa's wooden installation emphasizes the Gothic skeleton of the building.

Aula Magna di Ca' Foscari, Universität Venedig
Planpause Carlo Scarpas für die stereometrische Ansicht der Türwand mit Anlage der Fensterfüllungen und Türen
1955/56
Bleistift

Aula Magna di Ca' Foscari, Venice University
Blueprint by Carlo Scarpa of the stereometric view of the Aula door wall with window sashes and doors, 1955/56
Pencil

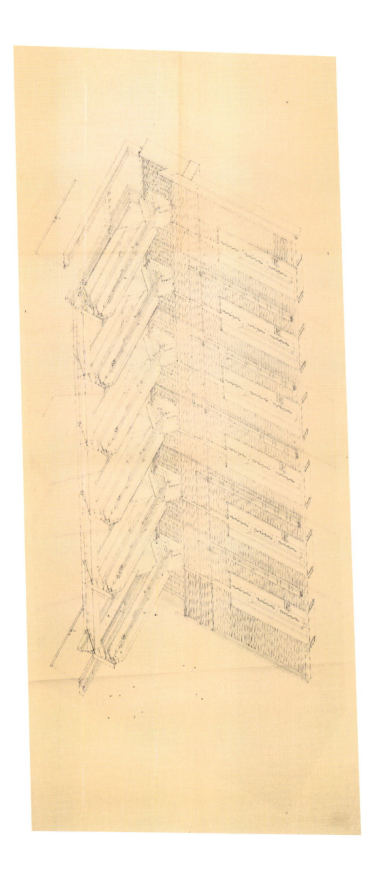

Olivetti-Schauraum, Venedig, 1957/58
Mit dem Gewinn des „Premio Olivetti" 1956 ergeht an Carlo Scarpa der Auftrag zur Gestaltung des Schauraums der Büromaschinenfirma Olivetti am Markusplatz, im Herzen Venedigs. Auf einem schmalen tiefen Grundstück in den Arkaden entlang des Platzes entwirft Carlo Scarpa einen Raum mit einer außergewöhnlichen Marmortreppe, die zu zwei balkonartigen Galerien führt. Der seitlich versetzte Eingang, die Skulpturen und das Wasserbecken leiten auf die – als neoplastizistische Dekonstruktion der Treppe Michelangelos für die Biblioteca Laurenziana in Florenz zu lesende – „Treppenskulptur" zu, die kaskadenartig hinabzufallen scheint.

Olivetti showroom, Venice, 1957/58
When Carlo Scarpa wins the Premio Olivetti in 1956, he is commissioned with the design of a showroom for the office equipment company in the heart of Venice on a narrow deep site behind the arcades along the Piazza San Marco. Scarpa suggests a room with an extraordinary marble staircase leading to two balcony-like galleries.
The entrance staggered to the side, the sculptures, and the water basin guide us towards the cascading "staircase sculpture" to be read as a neo-plasticist deconstruction of Michelangelo's staircase for the Biblioteca Laurenziana in Florence.

Olivetti-Schauraum, Venedig
Perspektive und Aufsicht der Treppe
mit Anlage der Abfolge der Stufen
1957/58
Velin, Bleistift

Olivetti showroom, Venice
Perspective and top view of staircase
with sequence of stairs
1957/58
Vellum paper, pencil

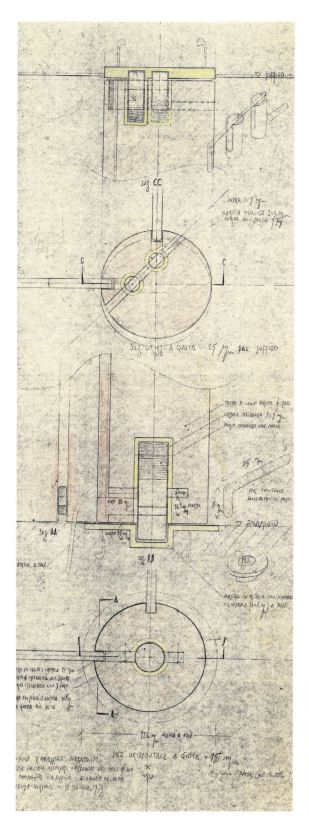

Villa Il Palazzetto, Monselice
Entwürfe für die Tür- und Fensterschließer
Februar/Mai 1974
Planpause, Bleistift, roter, blauer Buntstift

Villa Il Palazzetto, Monselice
Designs of door and window catches
February/May 1974
Blueprint, pencil, red, blue crayon

Villa Il Palazzetto, Monselice
Details der beiden Türen in Holz und Glas, die die Drehtür bilden, in Originalgröße, handschriftliche Angaben von Carlo Scarpa, 2 Vertikalschnitte der symmetrisch gedachten Türen
Januar 1974
Planpause, Bleistift, roter, gelber, blauer Buntstift

Villa Il Palazzetto, Monselice
Details of the two doors in wood and glass forming the revolving door in their original dimensions, handwritten notes by Carlo Scarpa, 2 vertical sections of the symmetric doors
January 1974
Blueprint, pencil, red, yellow, blue crayon

Villa Il Palazzetto, Monselice
Detailzeichnung der Türen und Fenster mit Beschlägen, in Querschnitt und Aufsicht
13. Mai 1974
Planpause mit Korrekturen mit Bleistift, rotem, gelbem Buntstift

Villa Il Palazzetto, Monselice
Detail drawing of doors and windows with fittings, cross-section and top view
May 13, 1974
Blueprint with revisions
(pencil, red, yellow crayon)

Villen / Innenraumgestaltungen   36

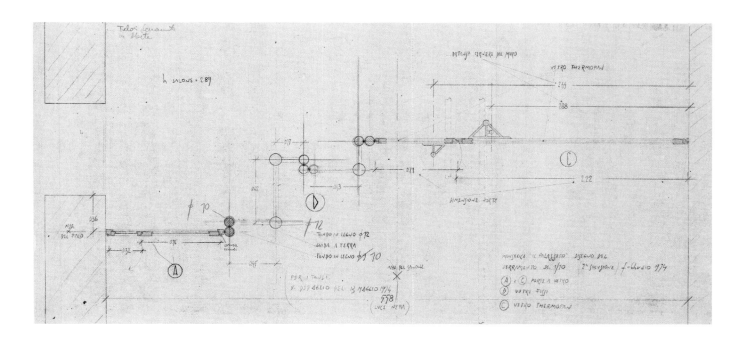

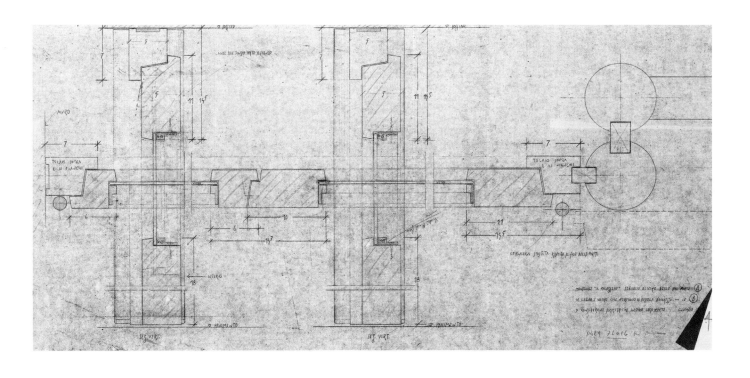

Die Architektur Carlo Scarpas

Tadao Ando

Mit Carlo Scarpa kam ich erstmals durch eine Fotografie der Fassade des Gavina-Geschäfts in Berührung. In einer beeindruckenden italienischen Stadtlandschaft war vor einer Außenwand eine gewaltige Stahlbetonplatte angebracht worden, die zwei auf die Öffnungen des Gebäudes Bezug nehmende symbolische Durchlässe mit Kreismotiven aufwies.
Darin bestand der Umbau. Die banale Fassade des bestehenden Gebäudes hatte eine beredte Wucht verliehen bekommen. Die Arbeit, die ein großes, unbeschränktes planerisches Geschick zeigte, und die schöne Aquarellskizze, welche die Fotografie begleitete, beeindruckten mich auf eine ganz andere Art als andere Arbeiten moderner Architektur dieser Zeit.
Scarpa wird im Allgemeinen als Architekt der stolzen Isolation gesehen, der auf Grundlage traditionellen Wissens durch den sorgfältigen Umgang mit Materialien und durch auf handwerklichen Traditionen beruhende subtile Details in einem Zeitalter moderner Architektur ein von Hand und Auge bestimmtes Bauen wiederbelebte. Ich habe viel von Scarpas Details gelernt, deren Palette von Entwürfen für Handläufe und Metallarbeiten bis zur individuellen Verlegung von Bodenplatten reicht.
Bei jedem Besuch des Castelvecchio in Verona oder der Querini Stampalia in Venedig entdecke ich neue Dinge, die mich beeindrucken. Selbst ein einfacher Wasserlauf ist so angelegt, dass er nicht bloß funktional ist; unaufdringliche Maßnahmen lassen das Fließen des Wassers hervortreten. Es sind genau diese subtilen Beziehungen zwischen Funktion und Ausdruck, die architektonische Details so faszinierend machen.
Scarpa unterscheidet sich jedoch insofern von bloß kunsthandwerklichen Architekten, als die architektonischen Elemente in seinen Arbeiten eine großartige Einheit ergeben, obwohl sie als unabhängige Teile zum Ausdruck kommen. Möglich wird das durch die Sensibilität und das planerische Können, mit denen er Objekten Form gibt.
Nur einige Projekte, an denen Scarpa im Laufe seines Lebens arbeitete, waren von ihm völlig neu entworfene Bauten. Wahrscheinlich ist der Brion-Vega-Friedhof, wo er ohne Einschränkungen planen konnte, deshalb ein trotz seiner geringen Größe so hoch konzentrierter vielgestaltiger Raum. Wie dies kein mächtiges symbolisches Bauwerk vermag, offenbart uns dieses kleine Werk, das uns Scarpa hinterlassen hat, die Wahrheit, dass große Architektur keine Sache des Maßstabs, sondern des Raumes ist.

The Architecture of Carlo Scarpa

Tadao Ando

I first learned of Carlo Scarpa through a photograph of the exterior of the Gavina Shop. An enormous reinforced concrete panel had been installed outside an exterior wall in an imposing Italian townscape, and two openings with circular motifs were symbolically arranged in that panel with due consideration of openings in the existing building.

That was the extent of the remodeling. The commonplace façade of the existing building was invested with an eloquent power. The work, which demonstrated great, unfettered design skill, and the beautiful watercolor sketch that accompanied the photograph impressed me in a different way from works of modern architecture of the same period.

Scarpa is generally viewed as an architect of proud isolation, who, by means of the skillful treatment of materials, backed up by traditional knowledge, and by fine details that made use of craft traditions, revived in a period of modernism an architecture designed by the hand and eye. I myself have had much to learn from Scarpa's details, from the designs of handrails and metalwork to the way floor panels are individually laid. I am impressed by new discoveries every time I visit the Castelvecchio in Verona or Querini Stampalia in Venice. Even a simple watercourse is designed to be more than functional; unobtrusive measures have been taken to make the flow of water more apparent. Such subtle relationships between function and expression are what makes architectural details so fascinating.

However, Scarpa differs from architects who are simply craftsmanly in that in his works, the architectural elements, though expressed as independent parts, together form a magnificent whole. The sensibility and design skill with which he gave shape to objects are what made that possible.

Only a few of the projects he was involved in during his lifetime were completely designed as new buildings by him. That is probably why the Brion-Vega Cemetery, where he was free to design without constraints, is such a highly-concentrated, variegated space, despite its small size. This small work left by Scarpa teaches us, as no enormous symbolic building can, the truth that the grandeur of architecture lies in, not scale, but space.

Museen / Ausstellungsgestaltungen
Museums / Exhibition Designs

Palazzo Querini Stampalia, Venedig, 1961–63
Die Restaurierung des Palazzos aus dem 16. Jahrhundert, der die Sammlung und Bibliothek sowie einen Vortragssaal der Fondazione Querini Stampalia beherbergt, nutzt Carlo Scarpa, um eine Neugestaltung des Erdgeschosses und des Zugangs vom Campo Santa Maria Formosa aus zu realisieren. Scarpa baut zurück, macht eine klassizistische Instandsetzung rückgängig, ohne zu rekonstruieren. Das Element des Wassers dominiert um und im Gebäude: Der „Portego", die Säulenhalle, wird in Steinkanälen entlang den Wänden von Wasser durchflossen; die Brücke über den Rio, aus der Mittelachse der Fassade gerückt, zitiert ostasiatische und venezianische Vorbilder.

Palazzo Querini Stampalia, Venice, 1961–63
Being entrusted with the restoration of the 16th century palazzo which houses the collection, the library, and a lecture room of the Fondazione Querini Stampalia, Carlo Scarpa grasped the opportunity to redesign the ground floor and the access from the Campo Santa Maria Formosa. He unbuilt the results of a classicist renovation without reconstructing anything. The element water dominates the immediate surroundings of the building and the interior of the building: it flows through the "portego," the columned hall, in channels of stone running along the walls, and the bridge across the Rio, off the central axis of the façade, hints at East Asian and Venetian models.

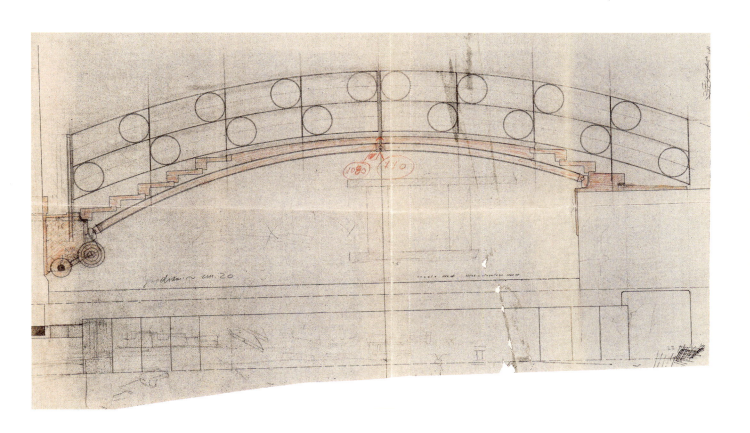

Palazzo Querini Stampalia, Venice
Sketch for the access bridge over the canal,
with pencil and crayon revisions and measurements,
scale 1:10
1961–63
Blueprint, pencil, red crayon

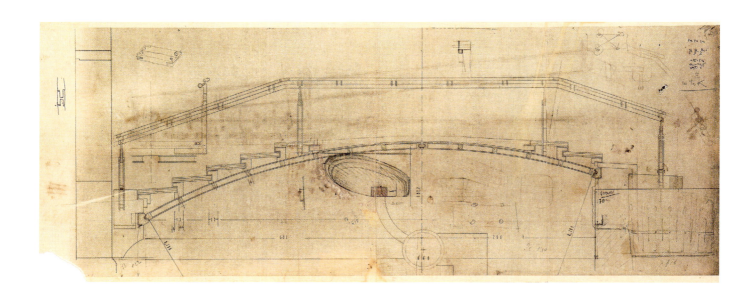

Palazzo Querini Stampalia, Venedig
Querschnitt der Form des Handlaufs der Zugangsbrücke, mit Material- und Maßangaben
1961–63
Entwurfspapier, Bleistift, orange, gelber Buntstift

Palazzo Querini Stampalia, Venice
Cross-section of form of access bridge handrail, with material specifications and measurements
1961–63
Sketching paper, pencil, orange, yellow crayon

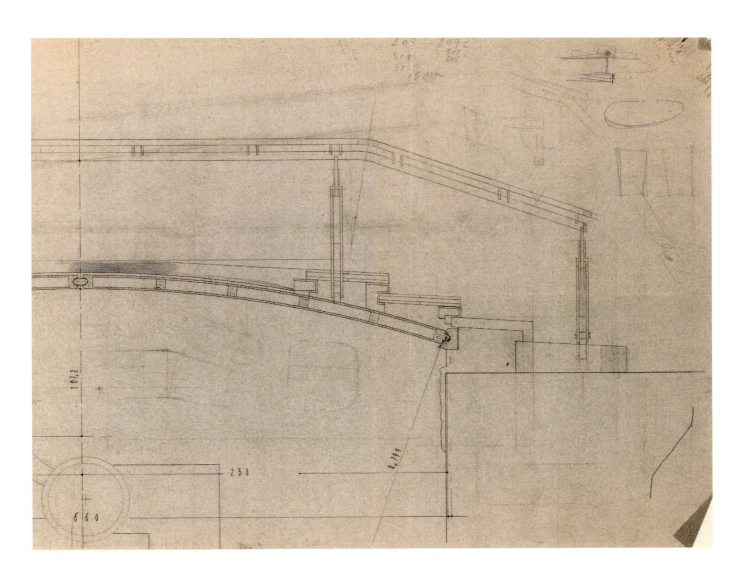

Palazzo Querini Stampalia, Venedig
Entwurf für die Brücke über den Kanal zum Eingang,
mit Maßangaben
1961–63
Planpause mit Bleistiftkorrekturen

Palazzo Querini Stampalia, Venice
Sketch for the access bridge over the canal,
with measurements
1961–63
Blueprint with pencil revisions

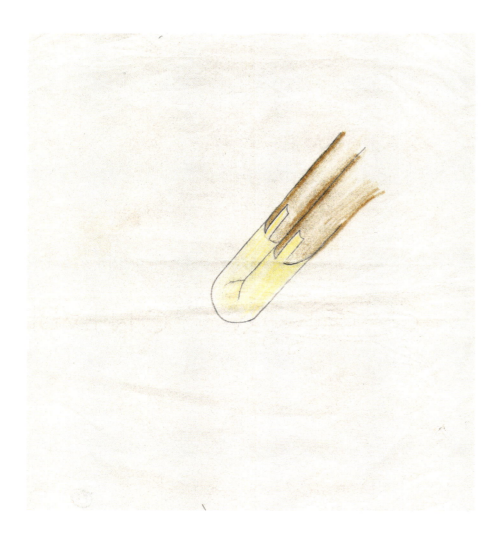

Palazzo Querini Stampalia, Venedig
5 Skizzen für den Querschnitt und die Form
des Handlaufs der Zugangsbrücke
1961–63
Velin, Bleistift, gelber, brauner Buntstift

Palazzo Querini Stampalia, Venice
5 sketches of cross-section and form
of access bridge handrail
1961–63
Vellum paper, pencil, yellow, brown crayon

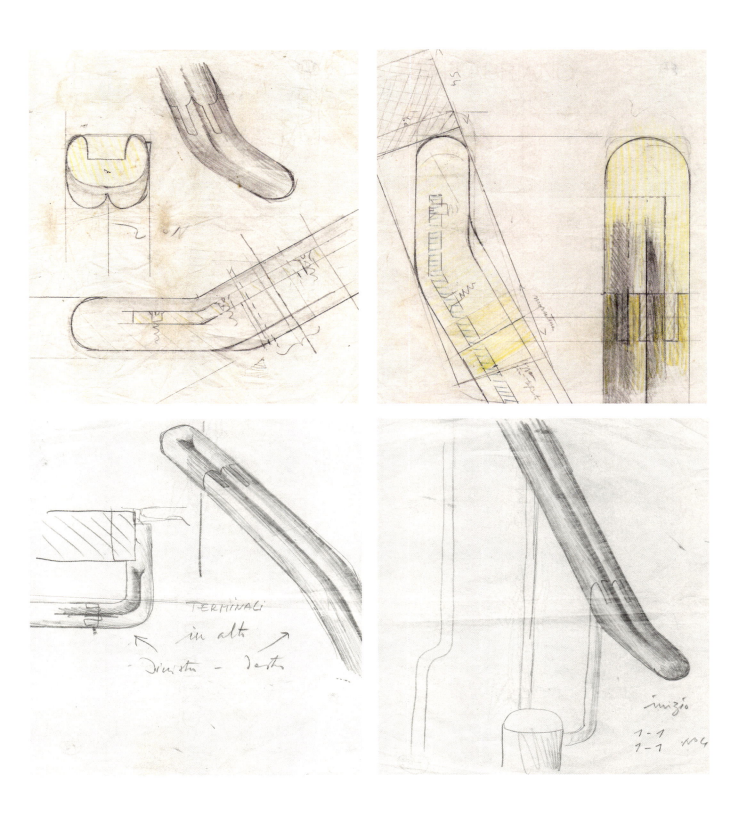

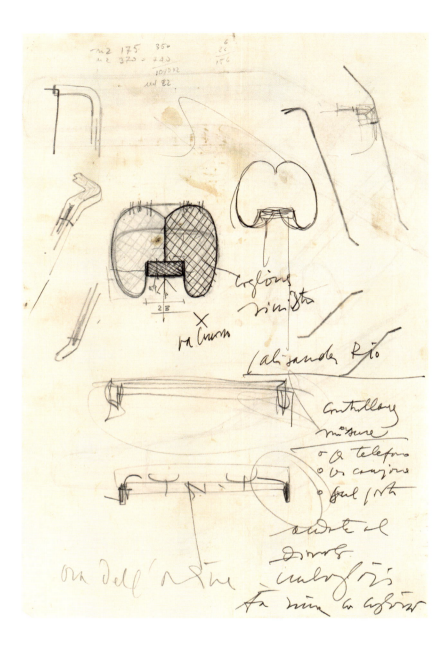

Palazzo Querini Stampalia, Venedig
Decke hin zum Kanal, Konstruktion, Querschnitte mit Maß- und Materialangaben, Maßstab 1:10
24. April 1963
Planpause nach Originalzeichnung Carlo Scarpas

Palazzo Querini Stampalia, Venice
Ceiling towards canal, construction, cross-sections with measurements and material specifications, scale 1:10
April 24, 1963
Blueprint after original drawing by Carlo Scarpa

Palazzo Querini Stampalia, Venedig
Doppelseitiges Blatt mit Skizzen für den Querschnitt und die Form des Handlaufs der Zugangsbrücke
1961–63
Papier, Bleistift, Filzstift

Palazzo Querini Stampalia, Venice
Sheet with sketches of cross-section and form of access bridge handrail, recto and verso
1961–63
Paper, pencil, felt tip

Palazzo Querini Stampalia, Venedig
Aufsicht der Brücke als neuem Zugang
1961–63
Planpause nach Originalzeichnung Carlo Scarpas, mit Bleistiftkorrektur

Palazzo Querini Stampalia, Venice
Top view of bridge as new access
1961–63
Blueprint after original drawing by Carlo Scarpa, with pencil revisions

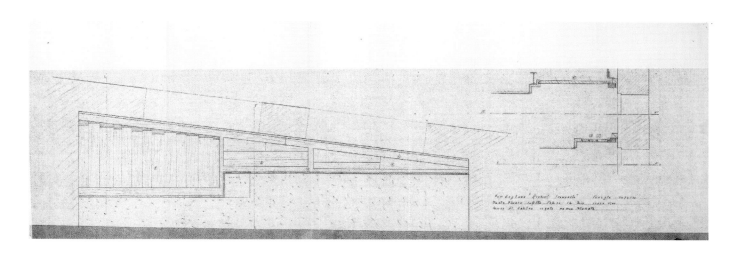

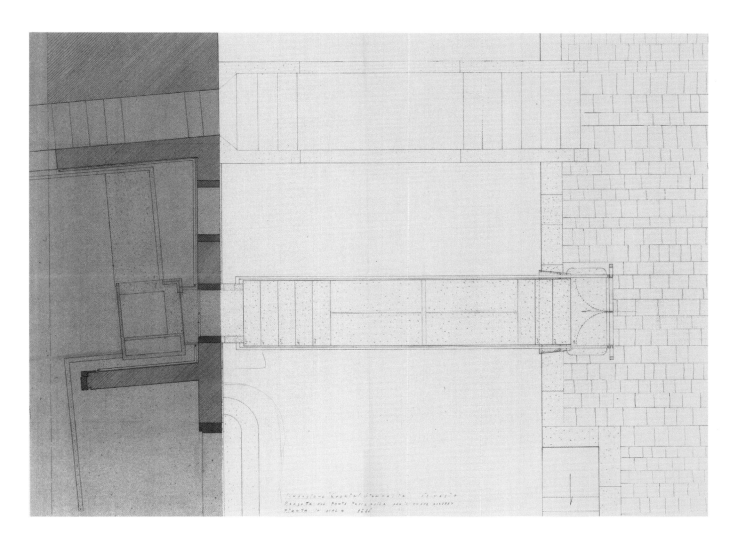

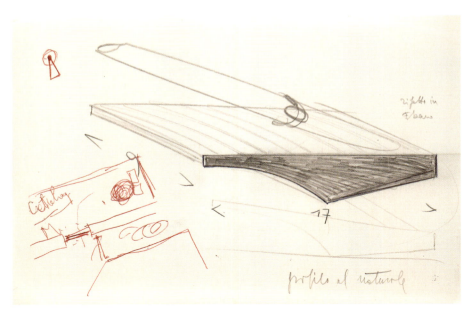

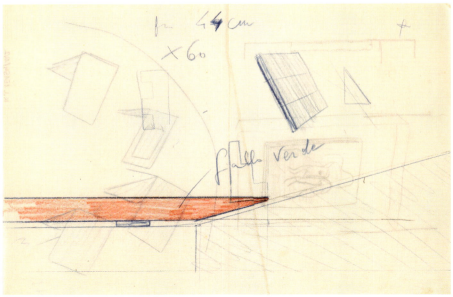

Palazzo Querini Stampalia, Venedig,
Tomba Brion et alia
Aus einer Serie von 35 Entwurfszeichnungen
mit Skizzen für Details
o. J.

Palazzo Querini Stampalia, Venice,
Tomba Brion et alia
From a series of 35 design drawings
with sketches for details
Undated

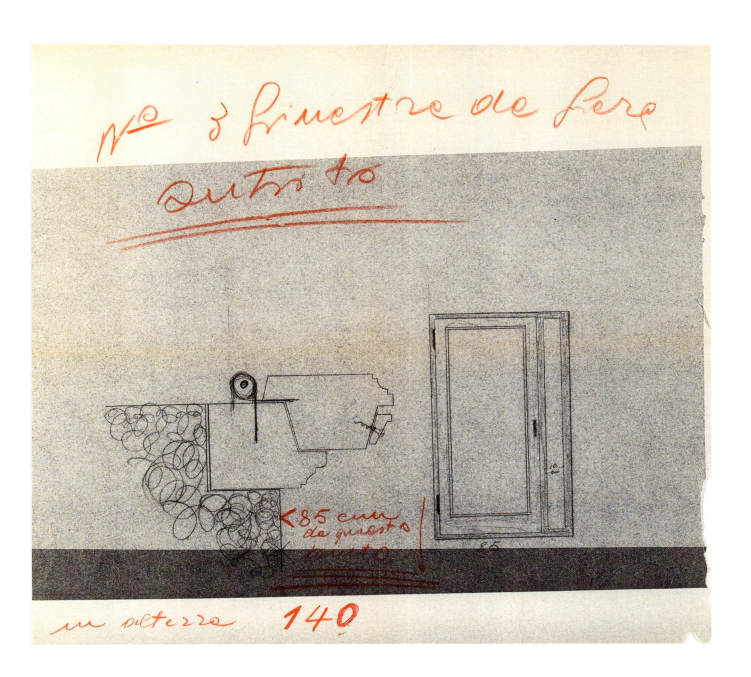

Palazzo Querini Stampalia, Venedig
Querschnitt der Fensterbank und Aufriss
eines Fensters, mit Maßangaben
1961–63
Planpause, Bleistift, roter Buntstift

Palazzo Querini Stampalia, Venice
Cross-section of window seat and elevation
of a window, with measurements
1961–63
Blueprint, pencil, red crayon

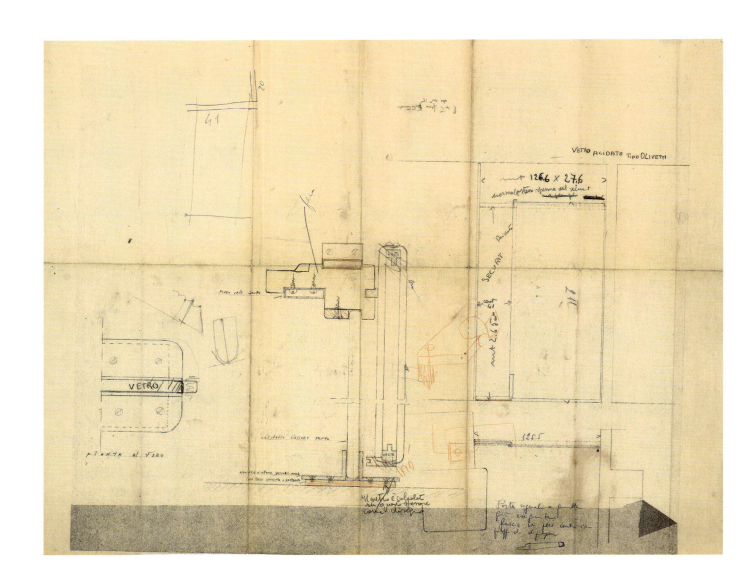

Palazzo Querini Stampalia, Venedig
Detailskizze für die Eingangstür, Profile der
Konstruktion, Querschnitte, teilweise im Original-
maß, sonst mit Maß- und Materialangaben
1961–63
Plankopie mit Zeichnung Carlo Scarpas,
doppelseitig, Bleistift, orange, gelber Buntstift,
Kugelschreiber

Palazzo Querini Stampalia, Venice
Sketch with details of entrance door, profiles of
construction, cross-section, either in their original
dimensions or with measurements and material
specifications
1961–63
Blueprint with drawing by Carlo Scarpa, recto and
verso, pencil, orange, yellow crayon, ballpoint

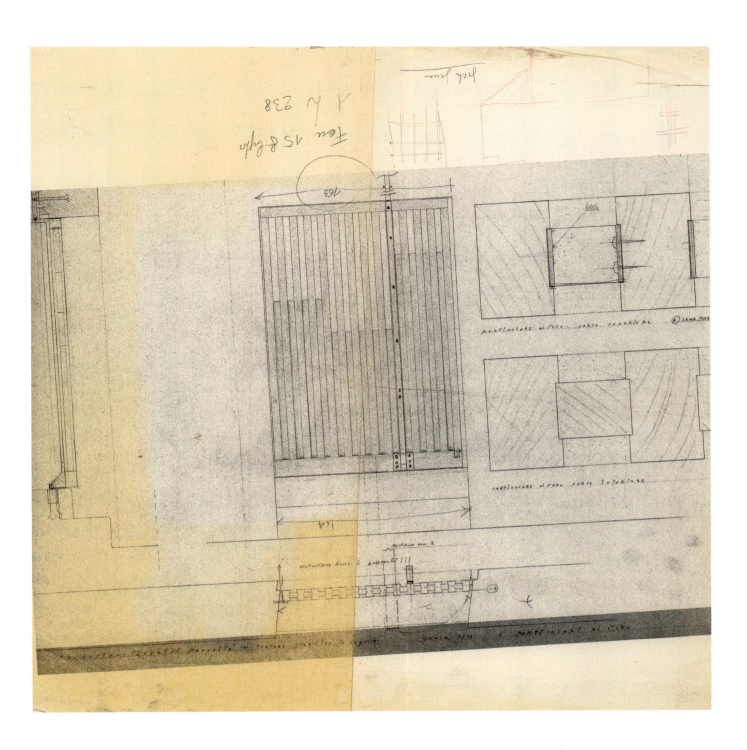

Palazzo Querini Stampalia, Venedig
Gartentür, Konstruktion, Details mit Maß- und Materialangaben, Maßstab 1:10 und Originalmaß
1961–63
Planpause, Originalzeichnung mit Bleistift, rotem Buntstift

Palazzo Querini Stampalia, Venice
Garden door, construction, details with measurements and material specifications, scale 1:10 and original dimensions, recto and verso
1961–63
Blueprint, original drawing with pencil, red crayon

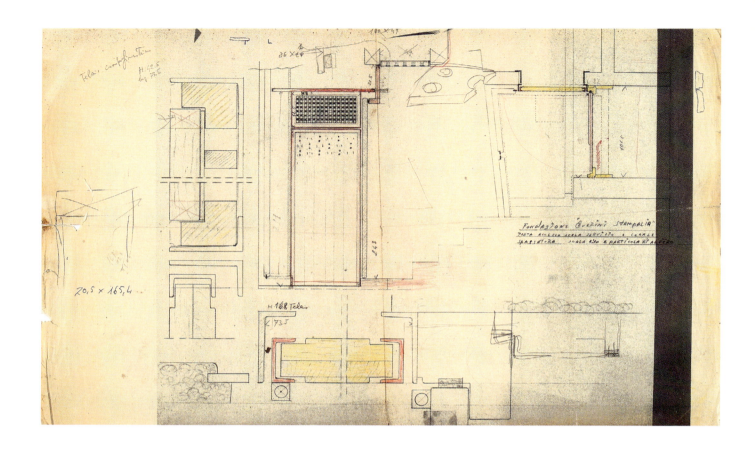

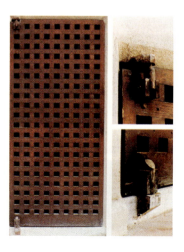

Palazzo Querini Stampalia, Venedig
Tür der Servicestiege, Konstruktion, Querschnitte
mit Maß- und Materialangaben, Maßstab 1:10
und Originalmaß
1961–63
Planpause, Originalzeichnung mit Bleistift, rotem,
gelbem Buntstift

Palazzo Querini Stampalia, Venice
Door for service staircase, construction,
cross-sections with measurements and material
specifications, scale 1:10 and original dimensions
1961–63
Blueprint, original drawing with pencil, red,
yellow crayon

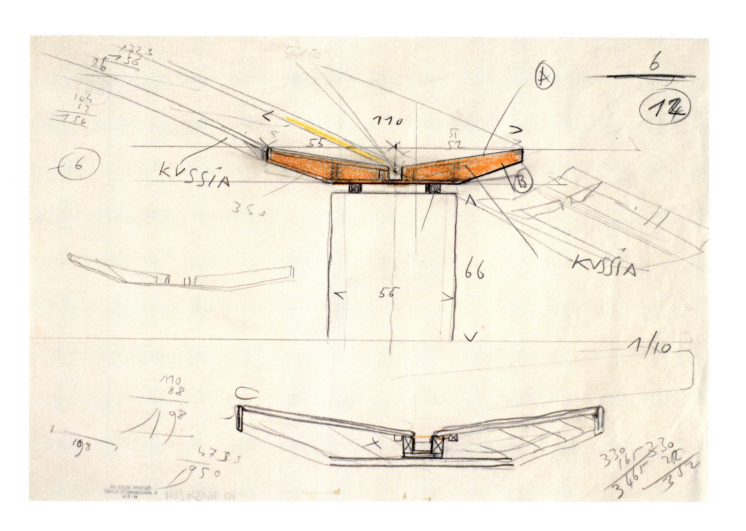

Palazzo Querini Stampalia, Venedig
Skizze für die Besucherbänke, mit Material- und Maßangaben
1961–63
Entwurfspapier, Bleistift, orange, gelber Buntstift

Palazzo Querini Stampalia, Venice
Sketch of the visitor benches, with material specifications and measurements
1961–63
Sketching paper, pencil, orange, yellow crayon

Gipsoteca Canoviana, Possagno, 1955–57
Anlässlich des 200. Geburtstags des klassizistischen Bildhauers Antonio Canova beauftragt die venezianische Sopraintendenza (Denkmalamt) Carlo Scarpa 1955 mit der Erweiterung des diesem gewidmeten Museums. Das im Heimatort Canovas, Possagno, zwischen 1831 und 1836 errichtete Gebäude ergänzt Scarpa durch eine lichtdurchflutete Halle für die Gipse und Terrakotten. Die aus und in die Ecken der Räume und der Decke eingeschnittenen Fensterschlitze und Glaskuben erlauben eine Lichtführung auf die in ihrer Position im Raum fixierten Kunstwerke, die „das Blau des Himmels ausschneidet", wie Scarpa selbst es definierte.

Gipsoteca Canoviana, Possagno, 1955–57
On the occasion of the 200th birthday of Antonio Canova, the Venetian Historical Monuments Authority commissions Carlo Scarpa with the extension of the museum dedicated to the classicistic sculptor in 1955. Scarpa adds a hall flooded with light for the plaster and terracotta figures to the building erected in Canova's home village Possagno between 1831 and 1836.
The window slits and glass cubes cut from and into the corners and the ceiling of the rooms provide a lighting focused on the fixed positions of the artworks – a solution that "severs a slice of blue from the sky," as Scarpa once put it.

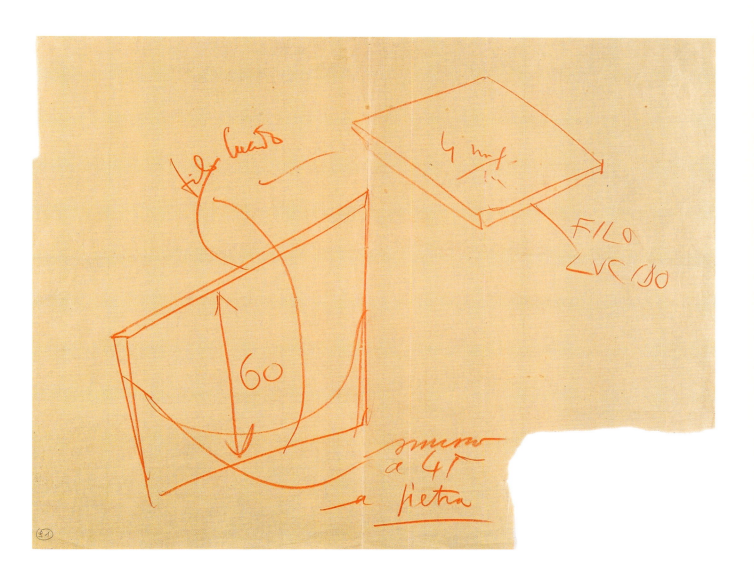

Gipsoteca Canoviana, Possagno
Querschnitte und Aufsicht der Böden mit Konstruktionsdetails und Form der Schrauben, mit Maßangaben, Skizze in Buntstift auf der Rückseite
1955–57
Beiges Packpapier, Bleistift, verso roter Buntstift

Gipsoteca Canoviana, Possagno
Cross-sections and top view of floor with details of construction and form of screws, with measurements, verso with crayon sketch
1955–57
Beige wrapping paper, pencil, red crayon on verso

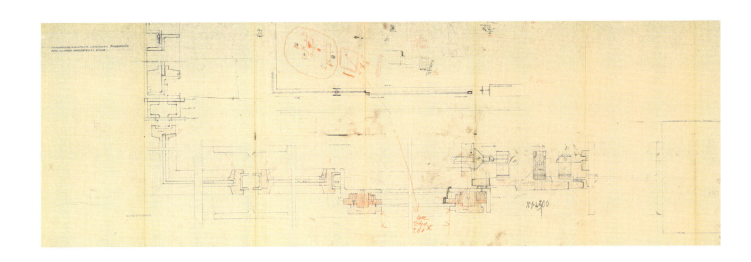

Gipsoteca Canoviana, Possagno
Querschnitte und Aufsicht der Profile der Türen
und Fenster, mit Maß- und Materialangaben
1955–57
Plankopie, Bleistift, verso roter Buntstift

Gipsoteca Canoviana, Possagno
Cross-sections and top view of door and window
profiles, with measurements and material specifications
1955–57
Blueprint, pencil, red crayon on verso

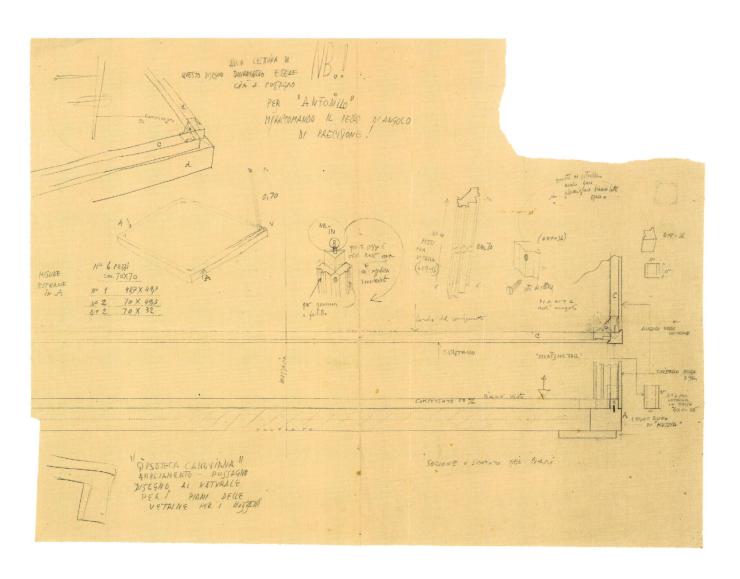

Gipsoteca Canoviana, Possagno
Cross-sections and top view of floor with details of construction and form of screws, with measurements, verso with crayon sketch
1955–57
Beige wrapping paper, pencil, red crayon on verso

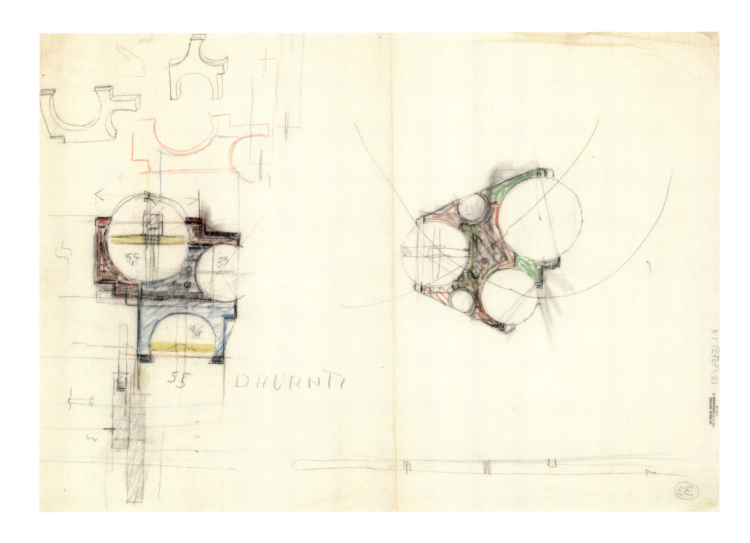

Waffenmuseum Castello di Brescia, Brescia
Detailzeichnung der Glieder des Treppengeländers
1971
Entwurfspapier, Bleistift, roter, blauer, grüner, gelber Buntstift

Museum of Ancient Weapons Castello di Brescia, Brescia
Detail drawing of banister elements
1971
Sketching paper, pencil, red, blue, green, yellow pencil

Waffenmuseum Castello di Brescia, Brescia
2 Entwurfskartons, zusammengefügt, mit maßgetreuen Details der Stäbe mit Gelenksverbindungen und Bohrlöchern
1971
Papier, Bleistift, roter, orange Buntstift, grüner Filzstift

Museum of Ancient Weapons Castello di Brescia, Brescia
2 sheets of cardboard, joined, with true-to-scale details of the poles, with joints and drill holes
1971
Paper, pencil, red, orange crayon, green felt tip

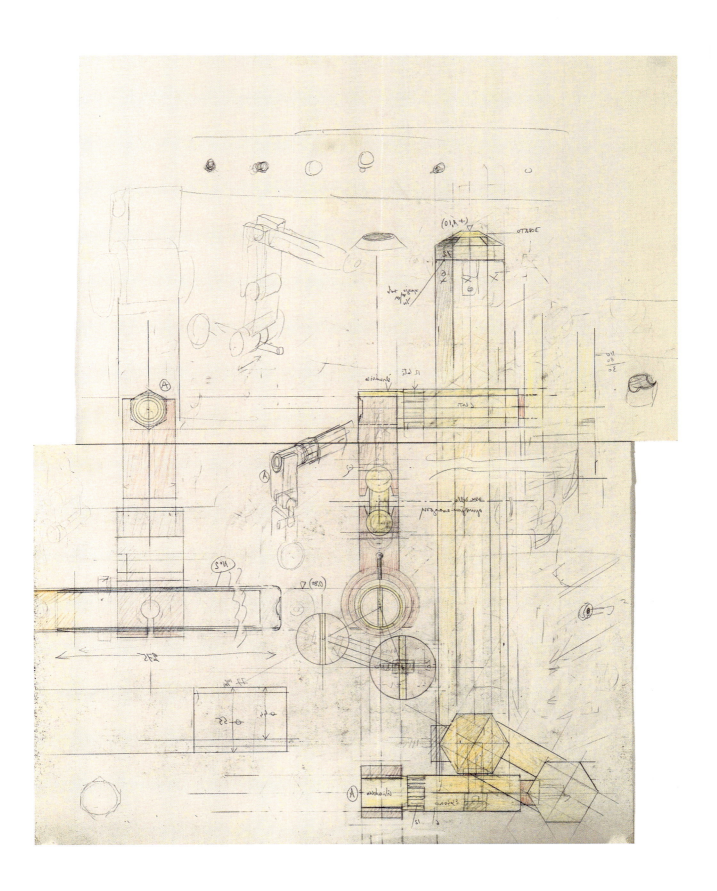

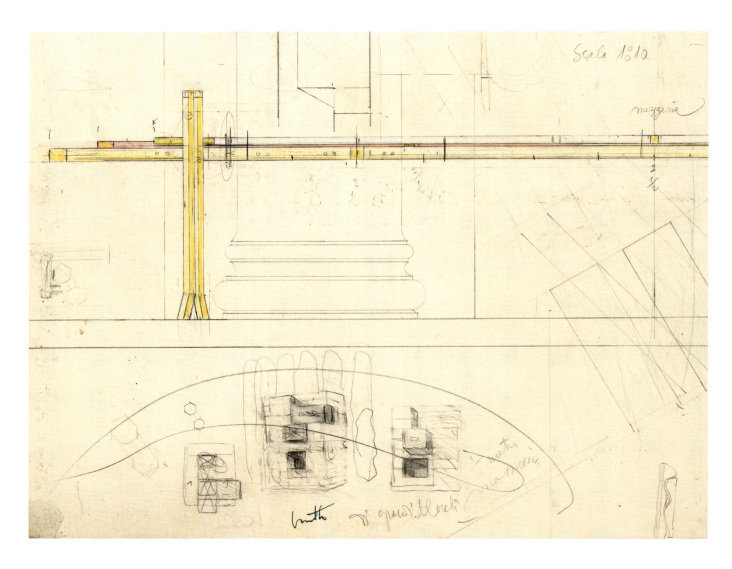

Piazza della Loggia, Brescia
Abspannung vor einer Säule, Maßstab 1:10,
unten Skizze eines Objekts, Hand und Kubus,
Entwurf für ein Denkmal
1975
Karton, Bleistift, roter, blauer, gelber Buntstift

Piazza della Loggia, Brescia
Anchoring in front of a column, scale 1:10,
below: draft of object, hand, and cube,
design of a monument
1975
Cardboard, pencil, red, blue, yellow crayon

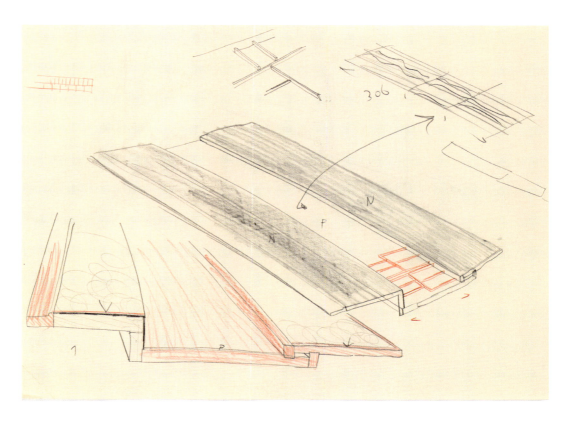

Museo di Castelvecchio, Verona
Skizze für die Besucherbänke
1956–64
Bleistift auf Papier, auf der Rückseite
auch roter Buntstift

Museo di Castelvecchio, Verona
Sketch of the visitor benches
1956–64
Pencil on paper, verso also with
red crayon

Museums / Exhibition Designs

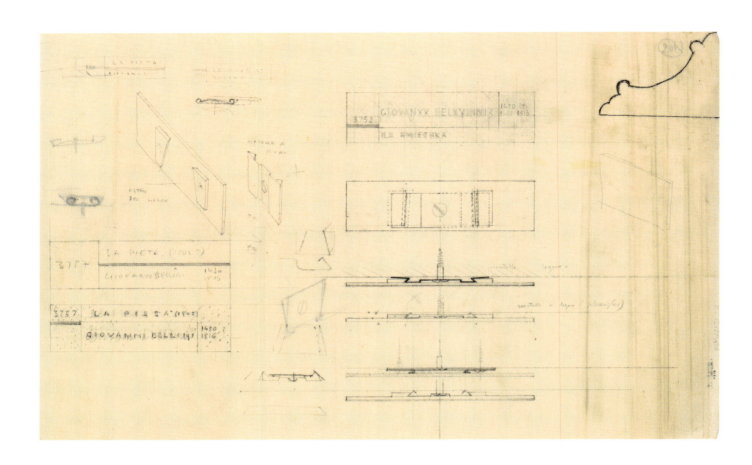

Ausstellung „Giovanni Bellini",
Palazzo Ducale, Venedig
Zeichnung für die Beschriftungstafeln,
Schriftproben, Materialangaben, Konstruktion
1949
Velin, Bleistift

Exhibition "Giovanni Bellini",
Palazzo Ducale, Venice
Drawing of text panels, type specimens,
material specifications, construction
1949
Vellum paper, pencil

Ausstellungen im Museo Correr und Palazzo Ducale, Venedig
Aus einer Serie von 52 Originalskizzen
Carlo Scarpas für Ausstellungsgestaltungen,
u. a. für die Neugestaltung des Museo Correr
und Ausstellungen im Palazzo Duacale
1949–59
Velin, Schreibpapier, Bleistift, roter, gelber
Buntstift, gelber Filzstift, Kugelschreiber

Exhibitions in the Museo Correr and the Palazzo Ducale, Venice
From a series of 52 original sketches for the
exhibition designs by Carlo Scarpa, such as
for the redesign of the Museo Correr and
presentations in the Palazzo Ducale
1949–59
Vellum paper, writing paper, pencil, red,
yellow crayon, yellow felt tip, ballpoint

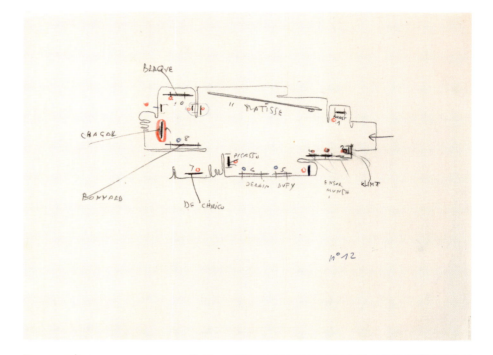

Palazzo Querini Stampalia, Tomba Brion et alia
Aus einer Serie von 35 Entwurfszeichnungen
mit Skizzen für Details
o. J.

Palazzo Querini Stampalia, Tomba Brion et alia
From a series of 35 design drawings
with sketches for details
Undated

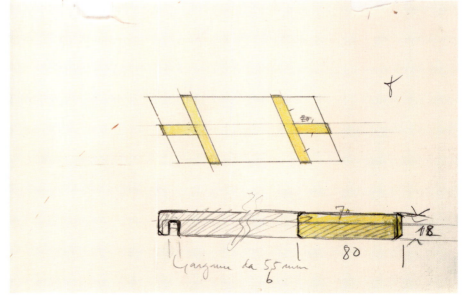

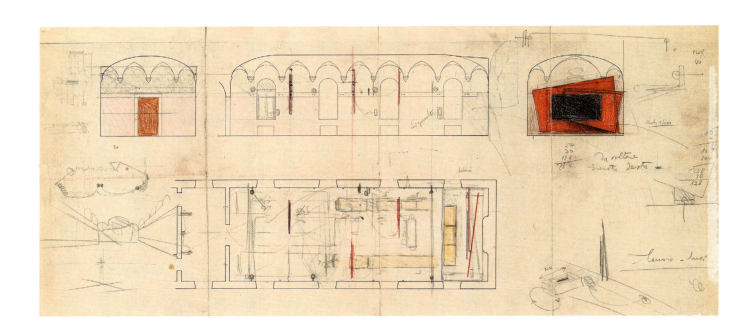

Architekturfakultät der Universität Venedig,
Aula Magna di Ca' Foscari
Ausstellungsinstallation, Aufriss, Wandablauf und Grundriss des Ausstellungsraums mit Anlage der Hängung der Gemälde, handschriftliche Vermerke
1960
Planpause, Bleistift, blauer, roter, orange, rosa Buntstift

Department of Architecture at the Venice University, Aula Magna di Ca' Foscari
Exhibition installation, elevation, wall sequence and ground plan of exhibition space with details concerning the hanging of the paintings, handwritten notes
1960
Blueprint, pencil, blue, red, orange, pink crayon

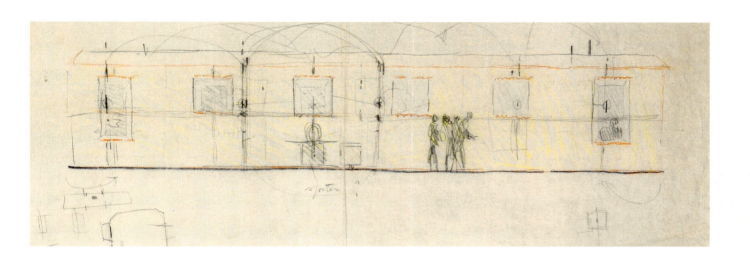

Architekturfakultät der Universität Venedig,
Aula Magna di Ca' Foscari
Ausstellungsinstallation, Entwurf für den Wandablauf mit angedeuteter Hängung der Gemälde und mit Besuchern
1954–56
Entwurfspapier, Bleistift, orange, gelber, blauer Buntstift

Department of Architecture at the Venice University, Aula Magna di Ca' Foscari
Exhibition installation design for wall sequence with outlines of the hanging of the paintings and with visitors
1954–56
Sketching paper, pencil, orange, yellow, blue crayon

Der letzte Traum

Arata Isozaki

Als ich vom plötzlichen Tod Carlo Scarpas in der japanischen Stadt Sendai erfuhr, fragte ich mich – wie wahrscheinlich jeder, der Japan ein wenig kennt –, warum er ausgerechnet dorthin gefahren war. Ich hätte mich nicht gewundert, wenn er nach Kioto, Nara oder Ise gereist wäre, denn dort befinden sich die Schätze der traditionellen japanischen Architektur, Stätten, die man immer wieder besuchen kann, ohne ihrer überdrüssig zu werden. Sendai hingegen liegt am anderen Ende Japans und hat nichts aufzuweisen, was in architektonischer Hinsicht von Interesse wäre.

Fährt man jedoch von Sendai weiter in den Norden, gelangt man zu den Ruinen der im 12. Jahrhundert zerstörten alten Hauptstadt Hiraizumi. Die Vermutung, diese könne das eigentliche Reiseziel Scarpas gewesen sein, rührt mich sehr. Dieselbe Reise hatte nämlich Matsuo Bashô unternommen, der bedeutende Dichter, der im 17. Jahrhundert die poetische Form des Haikus zur Vollendung geführt hatte.

Bashô hatte bis zu seinem fünfundvierzigsten Lebensjahr in Edo gelebt, dem heutigen Tokio, im Kreise seiner zahlreichen Schüler und als relativ wohlhabender Mann. Er war ein sehr angesehener Meister des Haikus, jener Gedichtform, die mit siebzehn Silben ihr Auslangen findet. Um diese Kunstform vor seinem Tod noch weiter zu perfektionieren, gab er sein ganzes Vermögen auf und begab sich auf Wanderschaft. Er irrte von einem Ort zum anderen, und nur der Tod konnte seiner Rastlosigkeit ein Ende setzen. Er verließ seine Heimat, das Städtedreieck Kioto–Nara–Ise, und reiste in den fernen Norden Japans, der in genau entgegengesetzter Richtung liegt und damals als barbarisches Land galt. Hiraizumi, der nördlichste Ort, den er auf seiner Reise erreichte, war bis ins 12. Jahrhundert der Sitz einer Familie von Landedelleuten gewesen, die so mächtig waren, dass sie es sogar mit Kioto aufnehmen konnten. Und mit Kioto als Vorbild schufen sie eine Architektur, die, wenn auch in bescheidenerem Rahmen, die Formen und Stile der Hauptstadt übernahm und perfektionierte. Der Großteil der von ihnen in Auftrag gegebenen Architektur wurde jedoch durch Kriege zerstört. Nur ein Bauwerk hat überlebt: das Mausoleum, in dem sich die Sarkophage der Landedelleute befinden. Zum Zeichen des Ruhms und des Reichtums der Familie ist das Monument von Blattgold bedeckt, und mit Gold überzogen sind auch die Details und die Schnitzereien. Bereits zur Zeit Bashôs war rund um das kostbare Monument ein größeres Gebäude gebaut worden, um es vor den Unbilden des Wetters zu schützen. (In diesem Zusammenhang fällt mir ein, dass Marco Polo bei seiner Rückkehr nach Venedig festhelt, er habe in China von „Cipangu, der Stadt des Goldes", gehört. Möglicherweise handelte es sich dabei um genau dieses goldene Mausoleum, dessen Fama bis an seine Ohren gedrungen war.) Als Bashô diesen Ort besuchte, war gerade Regenzeit, und auch an diesem Tag regnete es. Er beschrieb die Szene in einem symbolträchtigen Haiku: „Vom Großen Regen / bleibt sie nun doch wohl verschont / die Goldglanz-Halle?" Indem man ein zweites, schützendes Gebäude rund um das Mausoleum gebaut hatte, hatte man es für die Ewigkeit bewahrt. Aber das Gedicht will noch etwas anderes besagen, nämlich dass der Glanz dieses kleinen Mausoleums, das im Zentrum einer im 12. Jahrhundert zerstörten Kultur stand, sich über Zeit und Vergänglichkeit hinwegsetzt.

Bei der Betrachtung von Carlo Scarpas Werken bemerkt man, dass er dieselbe Vorliebe für das Detail hatte, wie sie einem in einem Stadthaus in Kioto in jedem Winkel und auch im Garten begegnet. Die Kombination geometrischer Formen, die an den Details seiner Bauwerke auffällt, mag eine entfernte Ähnlichkeit mit Frank Lloyd Wright suggerieren – was nicht weiter verwundert, denn Scarpa achtete und verehrte den amerikanischen Architekten. Er meinte jedoch, Wrights Stil könne nicht als fernöstlich bezeichnet werden. Möglicherweise bezog er sich dabei auf Beobachtungen, die er bei seiner Reise nach Kioto an der japanischen Architektur gemacht hatte, und war zu dem Schluss gekommen, sein Werk sei dem Osten mehr verbunden als das des Amerikaners.

Meiner Meinung nach erinnern vor allem die Genauigkeit und die Sensibilität, mit der Scarpa verschiedene Materialien zu kombinieren verstand, an die sorgfältige Konzeption des typischen Kiotoer Stadthauses. Auch jene, in denen sich der Einfluss des *Sukiya* (des Pavillons für die Teezeremonie) widerspiegelt, weisen eine Kombination sehr unterschiedlicher Materialien auf, und die Verwendung verschiedenster stilistischer Elemente erzeugt den Eindruck eines harmonischen Zusammenspiels. Genau das scheint die Technik zu sein, die sich im gesamten Werk Carlo Scarpas wiederfindet, von den Anfängen bis zu den letzten Arbeiten. Und auf seinen Reisen hat er zweifellos festgestellt, dass es in diesem Winkel des Fernen Ostens zahlreiche namenlose Bauwerke gibt, die denselben Prinzipien gehorchen.

Das Licht des Veneto zum Beispiel, vor allem in den Innenräumen, hat meiner Meinung nach dieselbe Qualität wie das Licht im Inneren eines Kiotoer Stadthauses, wie es mithilfe des Gartens erzeugt wird. Dieses Licht gibt einem das Gefühl, man würde immer tiefer in den innersten Teil eines Raumes gezogen, dessen Enge absichtlich hervorgehoben wird. Schon mehrmals habe ich gedacht, Scarpas Liebe zum Detail, die Aufmerksamkeit, die er gewissen Dingen schenkt, etwa dem Murmeln des Wassers, den Stimmen der Vögel, den auf dem Boden liegenden Blättern, sei darauf zurückzuführen, dass die Städte des Veneto von demselben Licht durchflutet sind wie Kioto und dass die Innenräume hier und dort sehr ähnlich sind.

Für die Japaner war eine Reise immer auch eine Reise in eine andere Welt. Oft hatte der Reisende mit einer Menge Schwierigkeiten zu kämpfen, und es war durchaus nicht sicher, ob er heil wieder nach Hause gelangen würde. Auch Bashô war zu so einer Reise aufgebrochen. Er besuchte die Orte, die von den Alten in ihren Gedichten besungen wurden, auch wenn sie mittlerweile nur mehr Ruinen und nicht wiederzuerkennen waren, und gedachte dort der tragischen historischen Ereignisse, deren Bühne sie gewesen waren, um durch die direkte Konfrontation mit der Geschichte die Gedichtform, die er bediente, zur Vollendung zu führen. Und Hiraizumi war eines seiner ersten Ziele.

Ich habe keine Ahnung, was Carlo Scarpa auf seiner Reise nach Japan, die seine letzte sein sollte, eigentlich vorhatte. Aber die Tatsache, dass er denselben Weg wie Bashô nahm, löst in mir eine Reihe suggestiver Assoziationen aus. Wer weiß, ob das Ziel der Reise, die ihn so weit weg von zu Hause führte und mit seinem Tod enden sollte, nicht auch ein Bauwerk war, das genau wie das goldene Mausoleum in alle Ewigkeit funkelt und glänzt. Nachdem Bashô sein Reisetagebuch *Oku-no Hoso-michi* (*Auf schmalen Pfaden durchs Hinterland,* übrigens ein Juwel der japanischen Literatur) fertig gestellt hatte, brach auch er zu einer Reise auf, von der er nicht mehr zurückkehren sollte. Diesmal sah er jedoch nicht voller Vorfreude glänzende Bauwerke wie das goldene Mausoleum vor sich, sondern schuf wie besessen Bilder schwärzester Verzweiflung. Mit folgendem Gedicht verabschiedete er sich von der Welt: „Zu Ende das Wandern: / Mein Traum, auf dürrer Heide / huscht er umher." Vor seinem Tod lag Carlo Scarpa noch einige Tage in dem Krankenhaus, in das man ihn nach seinem Sturz gebracht hatte. Welche Träume mag er in seinem Krankenbett wohl gehabt haben? Sind ihm dürre Heide und Ruinen hinter dem Glanz des goldenen Mausoleums erschienen?

The Last Dream

Arata Isozaki

When I learned of Carlo Scarpa's sudden death in Sendai, Japan, I asked myself – as everybody who is acquainted with Japan probably did – why did Scarpa visit this city of all places? I would not have been surprised if he had gone to Kyoto, to Nara, or to Ise, where one finds the treasures of traditional Japanese architecture – places to be explored tirelessly again and again. Sendai, however, is situated at the other end of Japan and has nothing that would be interesting in terms of architecture.

Yet, continuing north from there, one reaches the ruins of the ancient capital of Hiraizumi, a center destroyed in the 12th century. The assumption that this may have been Scarpa's real destination touches me deeply since Matsuo Bashô, the outstanding poet who brought haiku to perfection in the 17th century, made the same journey.

Until the age of 45, Bashô had lived in Edo – today's Tokyo – amidst his numerous followers and as a comparably well-to-do man. He was a very distinguished master of the haiku, a poetic form making do with seventeen syllables. To further perfect this form before he would die, Bashô relinquished all of his belongings and took to the road. He roamed from one place to another until his death put an end to his restlessness. He had left his home region, the triangle described by the cities Kyoto, Nara, and Ise, and had gone to the far north of Japan which, even then, was regarded as a barbaric country. Hiraizumi, the northernmost place he reached on his journey, had been the seat of a clan powerful enough to be a match for Kyoto. Using Kyoto as a model, this clan's families created an architecture which, on a relatively modest scale, copied and perfected the forms and styles of the capital. Most of the architectural works they commissioned were destroyed in subsequent wars. Only one building survived: the mausoleum that holds their sarcophagi. Like the details and carvings within, the monument is covered with thick gold leaf emphasizing the clan's glory and wealth. A bigger building had already been erected in Bashô's days around the precious monument in order to protect the mausoleum from inclement weather. (This reminds me of Marco Polo's recordings upon his return to Venice. He had heard about a Chinese "city of gold" called "Cipangu." This remark may relate to rumors he had heard about this golden mausoleum.) Bashô visited this place in the rainy season, and he described the scene in a highly symbolic haiku: "Even the long rain of May / Has left it untouched – / This Gold Chapel / Aglow in the somber shade." The second protective building erected around the mausoleum, preserved the construction for eternity, but the poem hints at something else: The splendor of this small mausoleum, which constituted the center of a culture destroyed in the 12th century, transcended time and its fugitive nature.

When you regard Carlo Scarpa's works, you will note that he had the same love of details that one finds in every corner of a wealthy town house and its garden in Kyoto. The combination of geometric forms characterizing the details of his buildings might suggest a distant relationship with Frank Lloyd Wright – which does not come as a surprise since Scarpa respected and admired the American architect. Scarpa maintained, however, that Wright's style could not be seen as Far Eastern. Referring to his observations of Japanese architecture made on his journey to Kyoto, he had perhaps come to the conclusion that his work had more connections with the East than the work of the American architect.

I think that the precision and sensitivity Scarpa revealed when combining different materials especially remind one of the careful design of the typical Kyoto town house. His projects mirroring the influence of the *sukiya* (the pavilion for the tea ceremony) show a combination of various materials as well as the use of different stylistic elements to create a harmonious interplay. This very approach seems to recur throughout Carlo Scarpa's œuvre from the beginning to his last works. The traveler obviously discovered that there were innumerable nameless buildings based on the same principles in that corner of the Far East.

For me, the light in the Veneto for example, especially its interiors, has the same quality as the light in a Kyoto town house produced by its garden. One is drawn deeper and deeper into the innermost part of the rooms, the narrowness of which is deliberately stressed. I often thought that Scarpa's love of details and the attention he paid to certain things such as the murmur of water, the voices of birds, and the leaves on the ground, resulted from the fact that the towns of the Veneto are flooded by the same light as Kyoto and that the interiors of both places have many things in common.

For the Japanese, every journey was a journey into another world. The traveler was often forced to cope with many difficulties, and it was anything but certain that he would return home unharmed. Bashô had also set out on such a journey. He visited the places that the old masters had extolled in their poems even if the sites were in ruins and unrecognizable. Wanting to perfect the poetic form that he used through a direct confrontation with history, he mused upon the tragic events for which these places had provided a stage. Hiraizumi was one of his first destinations.

I have no idea what Scarpa had in mind when he set out on his journey to Japan which was to be his last. Yet, the fact that he took the route that Bashô had taken triggers several suggestive associations. Who knows whether the journey which led him so far away from home and ended with his death was not also a building that would glisten and shine to the end of time like the golden mausoleum? After Bashò had completed his travel diary *Oku no Hosomichi (The Narrow Road to the Deep North)* – a jewel of Japanese literature – he too set out on a journey from which he would not return. This time, however, he was not filled with excited anticipation of the splendid buildings he would set eyes on, nor did he imagine any golden mausoleum. Rather, he obsessively produced pictures of unsurpassably dark desperation. It was with the following poem that he said goodbye to the world: "Stricken while journeying / My dreams still wander about / But on withered fields." Before he died, Carlo Scarpa was laid up in a hospital where he had been taken after his fall. What did he dream of in his sickbed? Did he see withered fields and ruins looming behind the splendor of the golden mausoleum?

Tomba Brion

Tomba Brion, San Vito d'Altivole, 1970–78
Der Auftrag für die kleine Nekropole für die Familie Brion am Rande des Friedhofs von San Vito d'Altivole gibt Carlo Scarpa die Möglichkeit, einen Mikrokosmos der eigenen und historischen Bau- und Gebäudeformen zu entwickeln, vom Portikus zum Pavillon und zu dem Teich, vom „Arcosolium", dem Wandgrab der ersten Christen, bis zur Kapelle. Scarpa hebt in diesem Projekt alle Elemente seines Bauens auf, wendet ostasiatische und klassisch-antike Details an. Im Zentrum des von einer Betonmauer umfriedeten Grabbezirks stehen die Sarkophage der Auftraggeber. „Der Ort der Toten hat die Bedeutung eines Gartens", schreibt Carlo Scarpa selbst. Fast zehn Jahre lang arbeitet er an der „anderen Stadt", die schließlich auch zu seiner Grablege wird.

Tomba Brion, San Vito d'Altivole, 1970–78
The commission to build a little necropolis for the Brion family on the edge of the cemetery of San Vito d'Altivole provides Carlo Scarpa with the opportunity to develop a microcosm of individual and historical forms of building and building forms ranging from columned hall, pavilion, and pond to arcosolium (an arched niche the first Christians used as a tomb) and chapel. In this project, Scarpa sublates all elements of his building and employs East Asian and classical ancient details. His clients' sarcophagi are positioned in the center of the burial ground enclosed by a concrete wall. "The place of the dead has the meaning of a garden," Scarpa writes. The architect works on this "other city," which finally also became his burial place, for almost ten years.

Tomba Brion, San Vito d'Altivole
Entwurf für die Schiebetür aus Beton, farbig gefasst, Aufriss mit hinzugefügten Detailskizzen Carlo Scarpas zu den Griffen und den Beschlägen und Führungen, mit Maßangaben und Notizen Scarpas
1970–78
Planpause auf Papier, Bleistift, mit rosa, gelbem, orange, blauem, grünem Buntstift gehöht

Tomba Brion, San Vito d'Altivole
Design of concrete sliding door, elevation with added sketches of details concerning the handles, fittings and guides by Carlo Scarpa, with measurements and notes by the architect
1970–78
Blueprint on paper, pencil, heightened with pink, yellow, orange, blue, green crayon

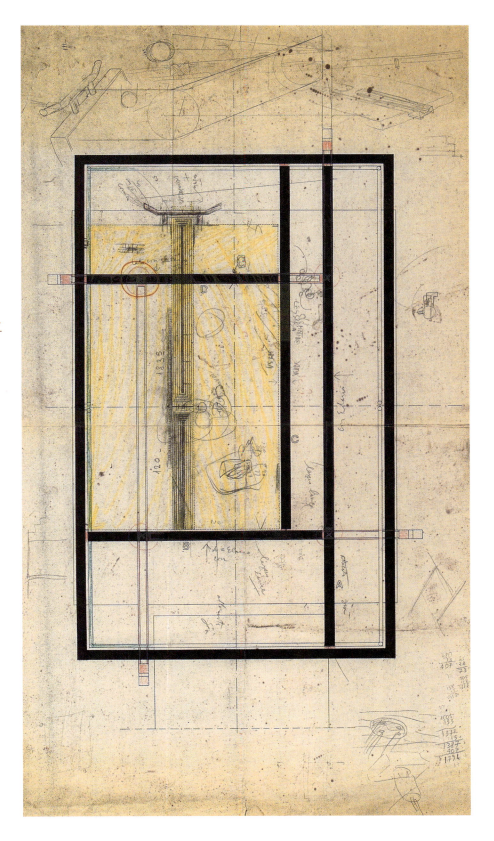

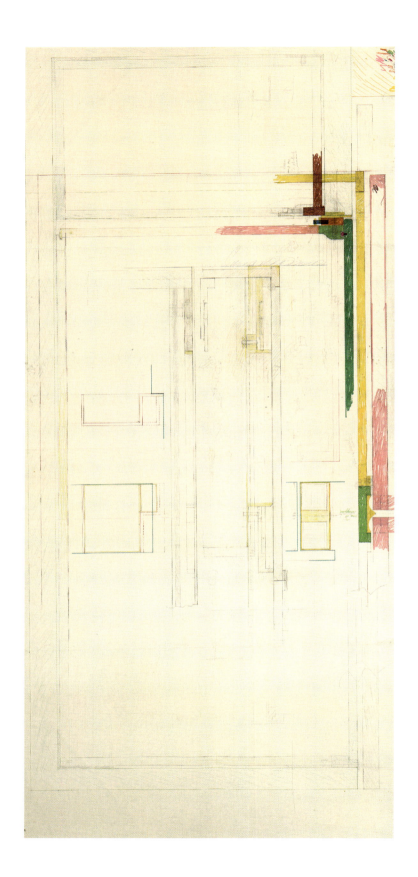

Tomba Brion, San Vito d'Altivole
Originalzeichnung für den Rahmen der Betonschiebetüren, farbig gehöht, mit Skizze einer weiblichen Figur, Maßangaben und Konstruktionsdetails
1970–78
Bleistift auf dünnem Karton, mit rotem, grünem, gelbem Buntstift und grünem, gelbem, rosa, orange, blauem, braunem Filzstift gehöht, ergänzende Bleistiftskizzen

Tomba Brion, San Vito d'Altivole
Original drawing of frame for concrete sliding doors with sketch of female figure, measurements, and construction details
1970–78
Pencil on thin cardboard, heightened with red, green, yellow crayon and green, yellow, pink, orange, blue, brown felt tip, additional pencil sketches

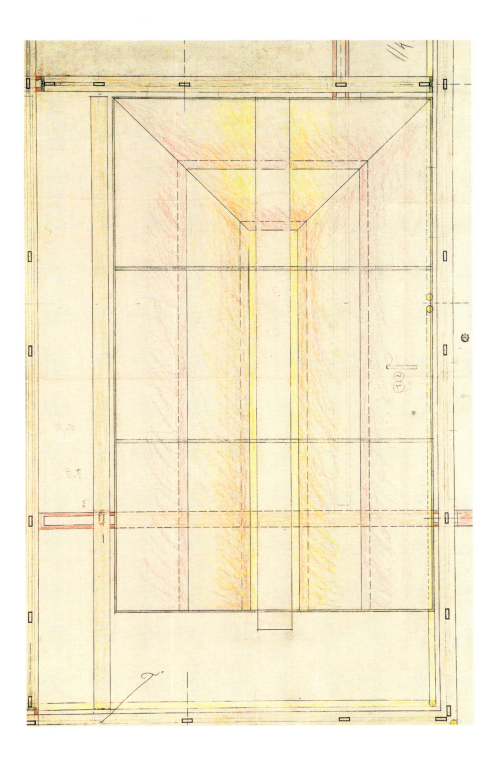

Tomba Brion, San Vito d'Altivole
Tür für die Kapelle, kolorierte Originalzeichnung,
mit Konstruktions- und Maßdetailangaben
1970–78
Zeichenkarton, Bleistift, roter, gelber, orange,
blauer Buntstift

Tomba Brion, San Vito d'Altivole
Chapel door, colored original drawing, with detailed
construction specifications and measurements
1970–78
Cardboard, pencil, red, yellow, orange, blue crayon

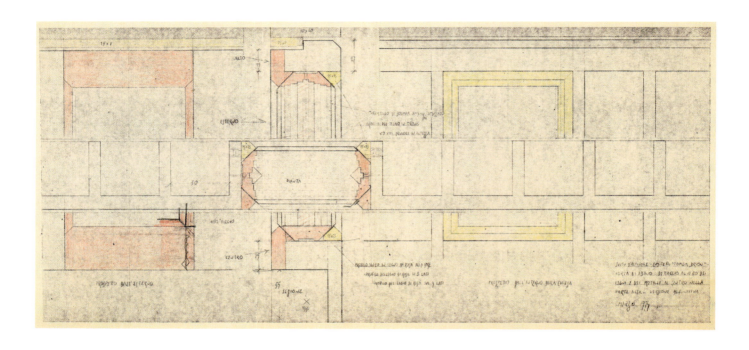

Tomba Brion, San Vito d'Altivole
Querschnitt des Rahmens und Aufbau der Tür der Kapelle aus Ebenholz mit Rosenholzeinlagen, mit Anlage der Messingtürgriffe, doppelseitig
März 1974
Plankopie nach Skizze Carlo Scarpas, Bleistift, roter, gelber Buntstift

Tomba Brion, San Vito d'Altivole
Cross-section of frame and structure of ebony chapel door with rosewood inlays, with brass door handles, recto and verso
March 1974
Blueprint after sketch by Carlo Scarpa, pencil, red, yellow crayon

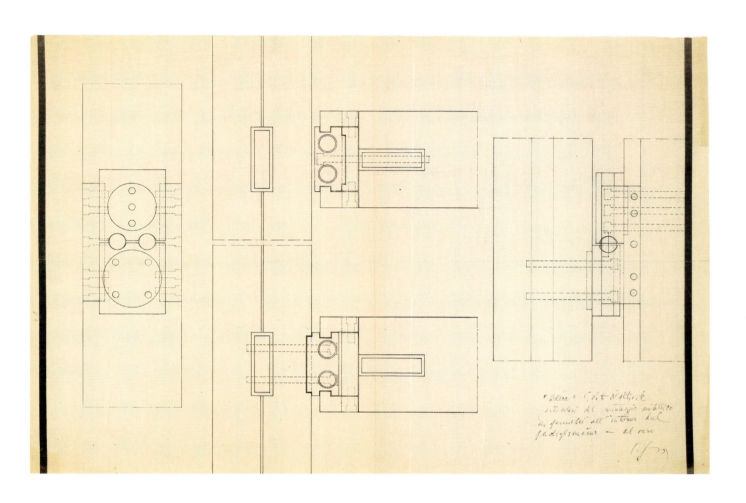

Tomba Brion, San Vito d'Altivole
Cross-sections of door hinges
1970–78
Blueprint on paper, colored with red, yellow,
blue crayon by Carlo Scarpa

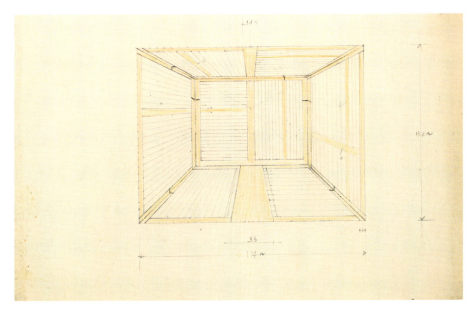

Tomba Brion, San Vito d'Altivole
Decke der Kapelle, Skizze aus dem Atelier
Carlo Scarpas, mit Maßangaben und Darstellung
der Struktur
1970–78
Karton, Bleistift, orange Buntstift

Tomba Brion, San Vito d'Altivole
Ceiling of chapel, sketch by a member of
Carlo Scarpa's studio, with measurements
and representation of structure
1970–78
Cardboard, pencil, orange crayon

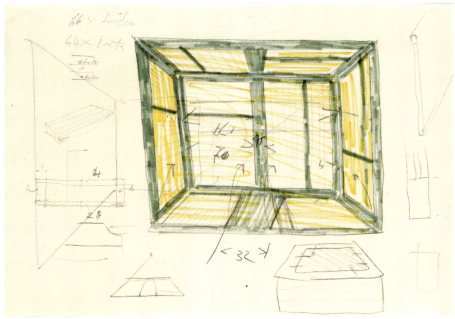

Tomba Brion, San Vito d'Altivole
Handzeichnung Carlo Scarpas für die
Flächenaufteilung der Decke mit Maßangaben
1970–78
Papier, Bleistift, grüner, gelber Filzstift

Tomba Brion, San Vito d'Altivole
Sketch by Carlo Scarpa for distribution of ceiling
areas, with measurements
1970–78
Paper, pencil, green, yellow felt tip

Tomba Brion, San Vito d'Altivole
Luster der Kapelle, 2 Kopfstudien, Originalzeichnung mit Maß- und Materialangaben
1970–78
Zeichenkarton, Bleistift, mit orange, gelbem Buntstift gehöht

Tomba Brion, San Vito d'Altivole
Chandelier of the chapel, study of 2 heads, original drawing with measurements and material specifications
1970–78
Cardboard, pencil, heightened with orange, yellow crayon

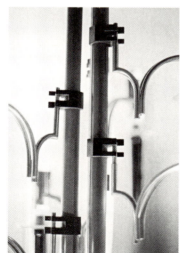
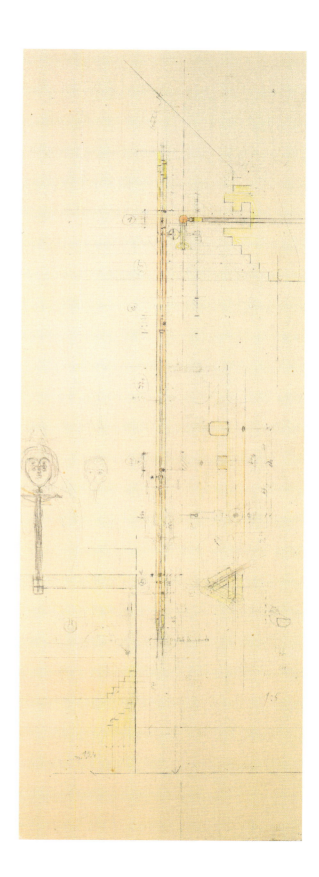

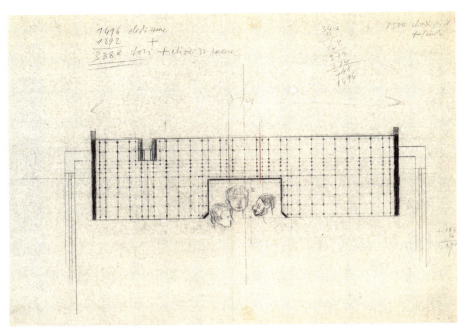

Tomba Brion, San Vito d'Altivole
Ansicht des Wandablaufs des Pavillons mit Skizzen
des Kopfes Carlo Scarpas, seiner Frau Nini und
seines Sohnes Tobia, mit Maßangaben
1970–78
Planpause, mit rotem Buntstift gehöht,
ergänzende Bleistiftskizzen

Tomba Brion, San Vito d'Altivole
View of pavilion wall sequence with sketches of
the head of Carlo Scarpa, his wife Nini and his son
Tobia, with measurements
1970–78
Blueprint, heightened with red crayon,
additional pencil sketches

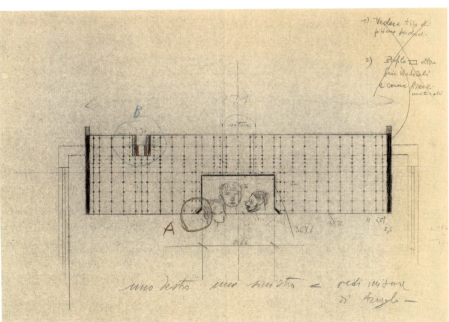

Tomba Brion, San Vito d'Altivole
Struktive Details und Maßangaben für den
Wandablauf des Pavillons sowie 3 Porträtskizzen
von Carlo Scarpa, Nini Scarpa, Tobia Scarpa,
mit handschriftlichen Angaben des Architekten
1970–78
Planpause auf Papier, Bleistift, roter, blauer,
brauner Buntstift

Tomba Brion, San Vito d'Altivole
Structural details and measurements for the
pavilion wall, as well as 3 portrait sketches of
Carlo Scarpa, Tobia Scarpa, with handwritten
notes by the architect
1970–78
Blueprint on paper, pencil, red, blue,
brown crayon

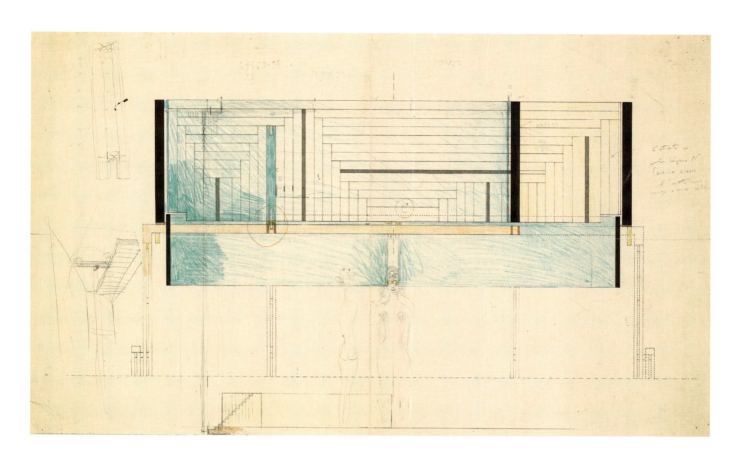

Tomba Brion, San Vito d'Altivole
Ansicht des Wandablaufs des Pavillons mit als „Modulor" genutzter Skizze einer weiblichen Figur, mit Maßangaben
1970–78
Karton mit Planpause, mit blauem, orange, gelbem, grünem Buntstift gehöht, ergänzende Bleistiftskizzen

Tomba Brion, San Vito d'Altivole
View of pavilion wall sequence with sketch of a female figure used as "modulor," with measurements
1970–78
Cardboard with blueprint, heightened with blue, orange, yellow, green crayon, additional pencil sketches

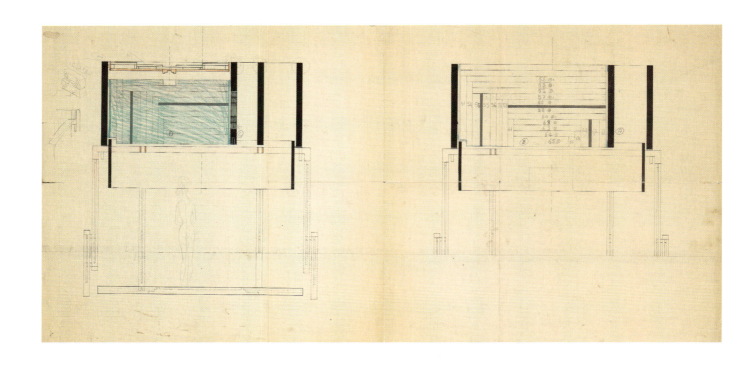

Tomba Brion, San Vito d'Altivole
Ansicht des Wandablaufs des Pavillons mit Skizze einer weiblichen Figur, mit Maßangaben
1970–78
Planpause, mit rotem, blauem, orange Buntstift gehöht, ergänzende Bleistiftskizzen

Tomba Brion, San Vito d'Altivole
View of pavilion wall sequence with sketch of female figure, with measurements
1970–78
Blueprint with revisions in color, heightened with red, blue, orange crayon, additional pencil sketches

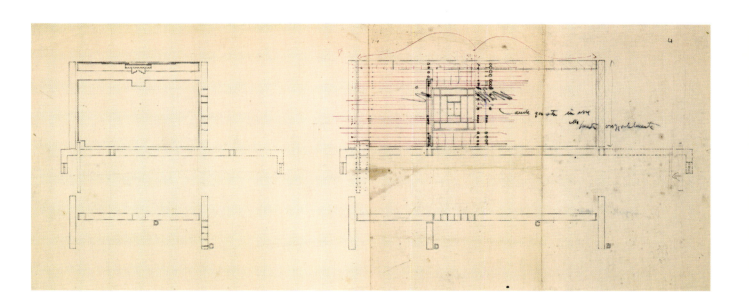

Tomba Brion, San Vito d'Altivole
Aufriss und Grundriss mit Maß- und Materialangaben
1970–78
Planpause, Bleistift, roter, blauer Kugelschreiber

Tomba Brion, San Vito d'Altivole
Elevation and ground plan with measurements
and material specifications
1970–78
Blueprint, pencil, red, blue ballpoint

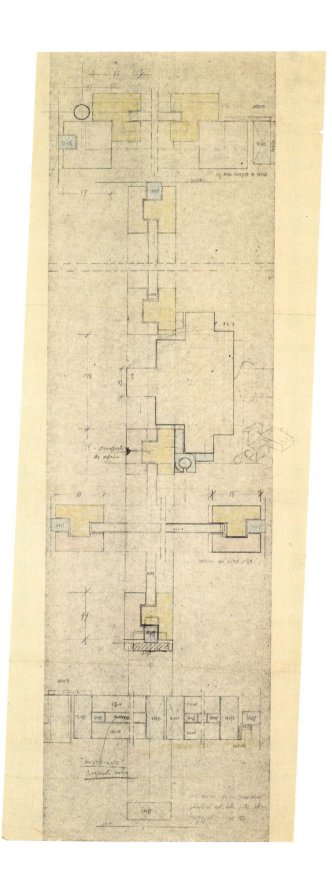

Tomba Brion, San Vito d'Altivole
Aufriss und Grundriss mit Maß- und Materialangaben
1970–78
Planpause, Bleistift, roter, blauer Kugelschreiber

Tomba Brion, San Vito d'Altivole
Elevation and ground plan with measurements
and material specifications
1970–78
Blueprint, pencil, red, blue ballpoint

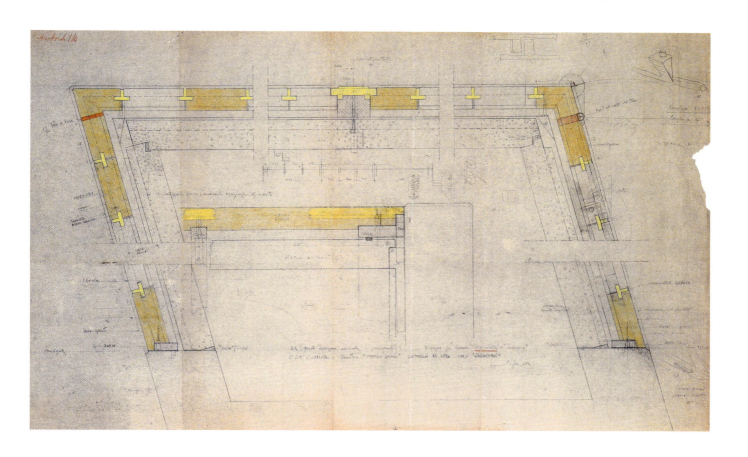

Tomba Brion, San Vito d'Altivole
Grundriss mit Maß- und Materialangaben,
Maßstab 1:10
1970–78
Planpause, Bleistift, orange, gelber, brauner Buntstift

Tomba Brion, San Vito d'Altivole
Ground plan with measurements and material
specifications, scale 1:10
1970–78
Blueprint, pencil, orange, yellow, brown crayon

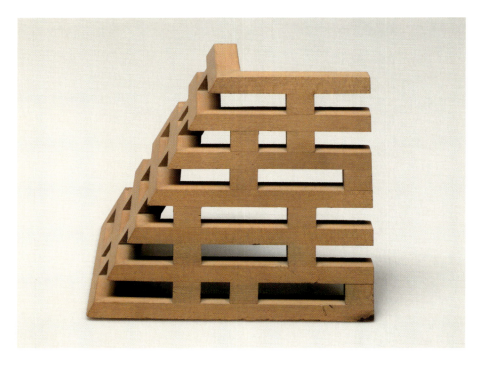

Tomba Brion, San Vito d'Altivole
Ecklösung der Umfassungsmauer
1970–78
Ramin

Tomba Brion, San Vito d'Altivole
Corner solution of walling
1970–78
Ramin

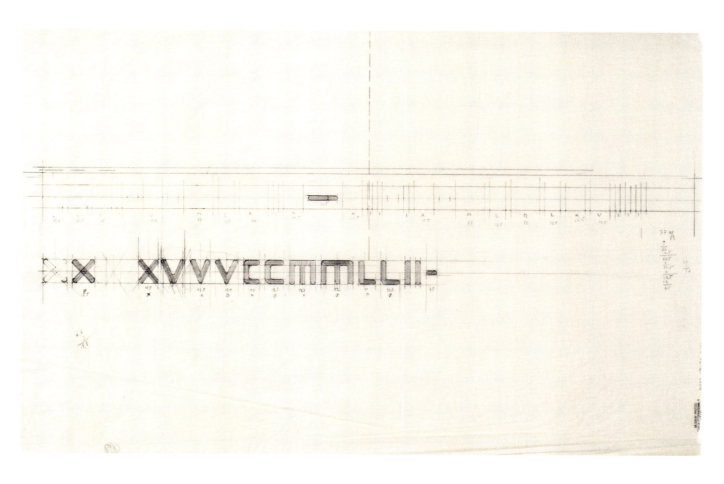

Tomba Brion, San Vito d'Altivole
Beschriftung der Sarkophage, Schriftprobe zur Umsetzung in Elfenbein, Originalzeichnung mit Maßangaben
1970–78
Velin, Bleistift

Tomba Brion, San Vito d'Altivole
Inscription for sarcophagi, specimen for execution in ivory, original drawing with measurements
1970–78
Vellum paper, pencil

Tomba Brion, San Vito d'Altivole
Inschrift im Sarkophagdeckel
1970–78
Makassar-Ebenholz, Einsatzstücke aus Elfenbein

Tomba Brion, San Vito d'Altivole
Inscription for sarcophagus lid
1970–78
Makassar ebony with ivory inlays

Tomba Brion, San Vito d'Altivole
Details der Innengestaltung der Kassette
für das Kruzifix der Kappelle
1970–78
Velin, Bleistift

Tomba Brion, San Vito d'Altivole
Details of interior design of the crucifix box
for the chapel
1970–78
Vellum paper, pencil

Tomba Brion, San Vito d'Altivole
Kassette zum Kruzifix
1970–78
Weichholz, Fichte

Tomba Brion, San Vito d'Altivole
Crucifix box
1970–78
Softwood, deal

Palazzo Querini Stampalia
Handlauf der Zugangsbrücke und
der Haupttreppe im Gebäude
1961–63
Ebenholz, geschnitten (1), Ramin (2)

Palazzo Querini Stampalia
Access bridge and main staircase
handrails
1961–63
Ebony, cut (1), Ramin (2)

Tomba Brion, San Vito d'Altivole
Holzpaneele, mit Einsatzstücken aus Metall,
mit Profilschnitten und Fräsungen
1970–78
Makassar-Ebenholz (1, 2), Metall, Fichtenholz (3)

Tomba Brion, San Vito d'Altivole
Wood panels, with metal inlays,
vertical sections and shapings
1970–78
Makassar ebony (1, 2), metal, deal (3)

Waffenmuseum Castello di Brescia, Brescia
Transennen des Treppengeländers
1971

Piazza della Loggia, Brescia
Gitter des Denkmals
1975
Ramin

**Museum of Ancient Weapons
Castello di Brescia, Brescia**
Transennae of banister
1971

Piazza della Loggia, Brescia
Bars for the monument
1975
Ramin

Tomba Brion, San Vito d'Altivole
Stäbe des Leuchters, mit Einsatzstücken
aus anderen Hölzern, gedrechselt
1970–78
Rio-Palisander (1), Makassar-Ebenholz (2),
Teak, Ebenholz (3), Birne, Ebenholz (4)

Tomba Brion, San Vito d'Altivole
Bars of chandeliers, wood with other woods
inlays, turned
1970–78
Rio rosewood (1), Makassar ebony (2),
teak, ebony (3), pear, ebony (4)

Die Werkstatt der Firma Giovanni Anfodillo & Söhne, Venedig
Workshop of the company Giovanni Anfodillo & Sons, Venice

„WIR WAREN EIN TEAM"

Carlo Scarpa und Saverio Anfodillo

Ein Gespräch

Ab den fünfziger Jahren arbeitete Carlo Scarpa bei der Umsetzung seiner Projekte mit der alteingesessenen Kunsttischlerei Giovanni Anfodillo & Söhne zusammen. Dies betraf alle wichtigen Projekte, die Scarpa von Oberitalien bis nach Sizilien realisierte. Die Werkstatt hatte sich auf Holzarbeiten und die Verbindung von Holz und Metall spezialisiert. Im Archiv der Firma, das 1999 vom MAK erworben werden konnte, haben sich Entwürfe aus der Hand Carlo Scarpas für Projekte aus rund dreißig Jahren erhalten, unter anderen für den venezolanischen Biennalepavillon, die Galleria Querini Stampalia in Venedig, das Museo di Castelvecchio in Verona und die Tomba Brion in San Vito d'Altivole. Aber auch Skizzen für Möbel zählen zum Bestand, etwa die Entwürfe eines Tisches für den mit Scarpa befreundeten Komponisten Luigi Nono oder des berühmten Tisches „Doge". Im Archiv befinden sich zudem Holzmodelle für Details des Hauses Zentner bei Zürich, für die Ummauerung der Tomba Brion sowie die Beschriftung der Sarkophage.

Die Zeichnungen, Pausen und Modelle sind Dokumente der engen Zusammenarbeit zwischen Carlo Scarpa und der Kunsttischlerei Anfodillo. Es handelt sich dabei um expressive Werkzeichnungen, die nichts von der strengen Reinheit von Architekturzeichnungen besitzen, die für Präsentations- oder Verkaufszwecke bestimmt sind. In der ihm eigenen Technik bereitete Scarpa alle Teile seiner Entwürfe minutiös vor. Einer ersten Zeichnung zum Verständnis folgte eine oft in Buntstift gehaltene Korrektur. Noch in den Pausen der Pläne korrigierte Scarpa vielfarbig, versah die Entwürfe mit handschriftlichen Kommentaren und erweckte den trockenen Durchschlag durch diesen Eingriff zum Leben.

Anhand der Modelle wird klar, dass Scarpa die Wirkung auch einzelner architektonischer Elemente am kleinen Holzmodell studierte, bevor er zur Realisierung schritt.

Bei einem Aufenthalt in Wien im Februar 2003, zur Vorbereitung der Ausstellung „Carlo Scarpa. Das Handwerk der Architektur" im MAK-Kunstblättersaal, sprach Saverio Anfodillo über seine Zusammenarbeit mit Carlo Scarpa.

Signor Anfodillo, erzählen Sie uns etwas über sich und Ihre Zusammenarbeit mit Carlo Scarpa.
Ich wurde in Venedig geboren und stamme aus einer Handwerkerfamilie. Schon mein Großvater führte eine Kunsttischlerei.

Ab wann gab es die Werkstatt Ihres Vaters?
Die Firma Giovanni Anfodillo & Söhne wurde 1938 gegründet. Sie wurde von meinem Vater geführt, der Carlo Scarpa ebenfalls kannte.

Und wo befand sich die Werkstatt Ihres Vaters?
In Venedig, auf den Fondamenta della Sensa, in der Nähe des Kinderspitals Umberto I, nicht weit vom Bahnhof, in einem typischen Handwerkerviertel.

Wann haben Sie begonnen, mit Ihrem Vater zu arbeiten?
Im Jahr 1950, unmittelbar nachdem ich meine Ausbildung beendet hatte. Und genau zu jener Zeit habe ich auch Carlo Scarpa kennen gelernt. Unsere erste gemeinsame Arbeit war die Gestaltung des Palazzo Abatellis in Palermo 1953. Für damalige Verhältnisse war das ein schwieriger Auftrag, der Transport der Holzteile von Venedig nach Palermo mit dem Lastwagen unserer Firma war eine Weltreise. Die Straßen waren schlecht und wir hatten eine Reifenpanne, aber Carlo Scarpa wollte die von ihm entworfenen Details nur von uns ausführen lassen – und so mussten sie nach Palermo transportiert werden.

Wie sah die Zusammenarbeit mit Carlo Scarpa aus?
Nun, Professor Scarpa ist zu uns in die Werkstatt gekommen, hat uns erklärt, was wir tun und welche Materialien wir verwenden sollten. Mir war von Anfang an klar, dass er ein profundes Verständnis des Handwerks hatte. Er kannte alle Materialien, die er verwenden wollte. Und auch mit Holz kannte er sich ausgezeichnet aus. Manchmal sagte er sogar zu mir, schau, dieses Holz möchte ich auf eine ganz bestimmte Art und Weise verwenden und bearbeiten, und wenn ich nicht ganz einverstanden war, weil dies unmöglich war, ließ er sich eines Besseren belehren.

Das MAK hat die Architekturzeichnungen von Carlo Scarpa, die im Laufe Ihrer Zusammenarbeit entstanden, von Ihnen erworben. Welche Funktion hatten die Zeichnungen für Carlo Scarpa und wie haben Sie sie verwendet?
Ich war begeistert davon, wie Carlo Scarpa zeichnete, nicht zuletzt weil er oft freihändig zeichnete, er hatte einen perfekten Strich – er war so gut, dass es fast aussah, als ob er ein Bild malte. Und eigentlich konnte man davon ausgehen, dass bereits die erste Zeichnung passte. Aber da wir uns immer lange über ein Projekt oder ein zu lösendes Gestaltungsproblem unterhielten, konnte es auch vorkommen, dass er nicht nur eine Zeichnung, sondern drei, vier, fünf zum selben Thema anfertigte. Und wenn wir nicht irgendwann die zuletzt entstandene Zeichnung zur Ausführung herangezogen hätten, hätte Scarpa die schließlich gefundene Lösung in neuen Zeichnungen immer weiter entwickelt.

Sie haben mir einmal erzählt, dass Carlo Scarpa Sie oft gebeten habe, länger in der Werkstatt zu bleiben.
Er kam oft zu uns in die Werkstatt, als die Arbeitszeit bereits vorüber war. Er rief an und sagte: Halt die Arbeiter fest, denn ich komme jetzt, und als er kam, bestand er darauf, dass die Arbeiter blieben. Und meistens erreichte er, was er

wollte, weil er so sympathisch und charismatisch war. Und wenn wir sagten: Entschuldigen Sie, Professor, aber die Arbeiter wohnen nicht in Venedig, sie müssen noch dreißig Kilometer nach Hause fahren, antwortete er: Nun komm schon, tu mir den Gefallen, schlimmstenfalls bringen wir sie mit dem Auto nach Hause. Und so blieben wir alle bis acht, neun Uhr abends.

> **Waren die Zeichnungen für Scarpa Kunstwerke oder Mittel zum Zweck? Er hat ja einmal gesagt, er zeichne, um die Dinge zu sehen, nur darauf könne er sich verlassen.**

Scarpa benutzte die Zeichnungen nur um uns zu erklären, was wir machen sollten. Er betrachtete sie nicht als Kunstwerke, er war ein sehr bescheidener Mensch und nicht der Meinung, etwas Außergewöhnliches zu tun – aber er mochte diese Art von Arbeit und war sehr sorgfältig.

> **Unter den Objekten, die das MAK von Ihnen erworben hat, befinden sich viele Pausen und auch Modelle. Welche Rolle hatten die Modelle, die Pausen?**

Carlo Scarpa fertigte Zeichnungen an, aber er bat uns dennoch, kleine Holzmodelle zu bauen, um ganz auf Nummer sicher zu gehen. Und wenn er das fertige Modell sah, sagte er, es ist in Ordnung, jetzt können wir fortfahren, machen wir uns an die Arbeit.

> **Auch für die Mauern der Tomba Brion sollten Sie quasi ein maßstabgetreues Modell aus Holz bauen.**

Um den Zement für die Umfassungsmauern der Tomba Brion zu gießen, hat der Professor von uns verlangt, dass wir Schalungen aus Tannenholz herstellen. Er hat mich regelrecht beschworen: Bitte, Saverio, das Holz darf keine Unregelmäßigkeit aufweisen, es muss ganz glatt sein. Stellen Sie sich vor, nur wegen des Zementgusses – daran sieht man, wie gründlich Professor Scarpa war.

> **Sie sagten einmal, das Material sei sehr wichtig für Scarpa gewesen, auch die Kombination von Holz und Eisen. Es gab eine Werkstatt, die für die Eisenarbeiten zuständig war.**

Die Schmiede, die Firma Zanon, deren Werkstatt sich ganz in der Nähe befand und die alle Eisenarbeiten ausführte, war ebenfalls mit uns und mit Carlo Scarpa befreundet. Wir standen immer gemeinsam an der Werkbank und unterhielten uns darüber, wie das Material zu verwenden sei, und über die Verbindungen von Holz und Eisen. Unsere Zusammenarbeit war überaus fruchtbar, denn es gab niemanden, der Befehle gab, und keinen Befehlsempfänger, wir waren ein Team.

> **Was waren die wichtigsten Projekte in Ihrer Zusammenarbeit mit Carlo Scarpa?**

Der Olivetti-Schauraum auf der Piazza San Marco, die Renovierung der Galleria Querini Stampalia in Venedig, die Tomba Brion: Das waren lauter bedeutende Projekte. Professor Scarpa hat dabei immer wieder verlangt, andere Materialien zu verwenden, er gab sich nicht zufrieden, er suchte ein Holz mit ganz bestimmten Eigenschaften, das eine ganz bestimmte Farbe hatte, und wir versuchten ihn zufrieden zu stellen. Wir haben in allen Lagern gesucht, um genau das Holz zu finden, das er verwenden wollte.

> **Sehr interessant ist auch, dass er immer auf der Suche nach neuen Materialien war.**

Ja, und ich hatte zum Glück Kontakte zu Lieferanten. Hin und wieder fanden wir neue, unbekannte Hölzer, und ich sagte: Professor, wir haben eine Art gelbes Holz gefunden – denn er wollte ein bestimmtes gelbes Holz –, und er sagte: Ich schaue es mir gleich an. Es handelte sich um Kussia-Holz [ein Tropenholz], das wir bei verschiedenen Türen des Palazzo Querini Stampalia verwendet haben, sowohl bei Ausstellungen als auch bei speziellen Details, in Verbindung mit Eisen. Darüber war Scarpa sehr zufrieden: Endlich habe ich gefunden, was ich suchte, meinte er. Aber er hat auch Kunstholz neben edlen Hölzern verwendet, wenn das seinen Vorstellungen entsprach.

> **Es gab also eine sehr enge Zusammenarbeit zwischen Architekt, Tischler und Schmied.**

Ja, wir arbeiteten immer zusammen. Aber der Professor war auch sehr sympathisch, obwohl er sehr fordernd sein konnte, denn er war bei Arbeiten oft zeitlich im Rückstand. Dann schickte er Zeichnungen, worauf geschrieben stand: Diese Zeichnung muss augenblicklich ausgeführt werden, hast du verstanden, Saverio, sofort.

> **Sie haben bis zu seinem Tod mit ihm zusammengearbeitet?**

Bis zu seinem Tod. Wir warteten ja darauf, dass er aus Japan zurückkehrte, weil wir ein gemeinsames Projekt hatten, und stattdessen erhielten wir diese schreckliche Nachricht.

> **Was war Ihr letztes Projekt?**

Die Tomba Brion, daran haben wir vier, fünf Jahre gearbeitet, das war unsere letzte gemeinsame Arbeit.

> **Wie lange haben Sie nach Carlo Scarpas Tod noch in Ihrer Werkstatt gearbeitet? Sie haben mit Ihrem Bruder zusammengearbeitet, nicht wahr?**

Ja, immer. Wir haben unsere Werkstatt 1996 geschlossen, vor sieben Jahren.

> **Sie haben mir bereits erzählt, dass die Arbeit in den letzten Jahren schwierig geworden war.**

Sehr schwierig. Venedig ist eine spezielle Stadt, es war unmöglich, die Werkstatt so umzubauen, dass sie die neuen Auflagen erfüllte. Wir hatten weder genug Platz noch die Möglichkeit, die Vorrichtungen zur Beseitigung von Dämpfen und Abfällen einzuführen, und so mussten wir uns entscheiden, entweder umzusiedeln oder zuzumachen. Letzten Endes haben wir uns fürs Zusperren entschlossen, denn auch wir hatten inzwischen ein gewisses Alter erreicht und unsere Söhne waren uns nicht nachgefolgt. Also haben wir gesagt, ist gut. Machen wir Schluss.

> **Sie haben gut dreißig Jahre mit Carlo Scarpa zusammengearbeitet. Worin bestand das Besonders daran?**

In seinem Temperament. Er war freundlich, er verstand etwas vom Handwerk, er schätzte unsere Arbeit. Er war immer freundlich zu uns und er hat niemals von uns verlangt etwas auszuführen, was wir nicht ausführen konnten.

Es war eher ein Vergnügen, mit ihm zu arbeiten, als ein großer Gewinn?
Um die Wahrheit zu sagen: Ich habe zwar viel gelernt und es hat mir auch großen Spaß gemacht, mit Professor Scarpa zu arbeiten, aber Geld haben wir bestimmt nicht viel mit ihm verdient. Denn oft genug mussten wir die Dinge zweimal, dreimal machen, bis das Stück, das er in Auftrag gegeben hatte, so perfekt war, wie er es sich vorstellte.

Ist eine derartige Zusammenarbeit heute noch möglich?
Leider nein, denn unsere Berufe sterben alle aus. Die Architekten haben heute eine andere Art des Herangehens, sie kommen mit fertigen Entwürfen, die sie lediglich umgesetzt sehen wollen. Und die Handwerker sind heutzutage dazu verurteilt, ihre Werkstätten zu schließen, weil die Handarbeit durch die Lohnkosten und die strengen gesetzlichen Auflagen nicht mehr bezahlbar ist. Heutzutage wird alles serienmäßig hergestellt, aber das Serienmäßige war nichts für Professor Scarpa. Die Sachen, die er machte, waren einzigartig.

Das Gespräch mit Saverio Anfodillo führte der MAK-Kurator Rainald Franz

"WE WERE A TEAM"

Carlo Scarpa and Saverio Anfodillo

A Conversation

Ever since the 1950s, Carlo Scarpa had been working together with the old-established cabinetmakers Giovanni Anfodillo & Sons to realize his designs. This holds true for all of his important projects carried out from Northern Italy to Sicily. The Anfodillo cabinetmakers had specialized in woodwork and combinations of wood and metal. The company archives acquired by the MAK in 1999 comprise drawings by Carlo Scarpa from three decades of work, among them, the design for the Venezuelan Biennial pavilion, the Museo di Castelvecchio in Verona, the Galleria Querini Stampalia, and the Tomba Brion. The archives also include drafts for pieces of furniture such as the designs of a table for the composer Luigi Nono, a friend of Scarpa's, or of the famous "Doge" table. There are also some wooden models of detail studies for the Zentner House near Zurich, for the walling of the Tomba Brion, and for the epitaph on the family's sarcophagus.

The drawings, plans, and models leave no doubt about the close cooperation between Scarpa and the Anfodillo cabinetmakers. The drawings are expressive working drafts having nothing in common with the austere neatness of architectural designs meant for presentation or to be put up for sale. In his characteristic technique, Scarpa meticulously prepared every single part of his designs. He often used crayons to correct his first rough sketches that were to just convey the gist of it. Scarpa corrected even the blueprints in different colors, adding handwritten comments on the plans, and thus imbued the sober copies with life. The models evidence that Scarpa studied the effect even of single architectonic elements in wooden miniatures before he started to realize his designs.

While preparing the exhibition "Carlo Scarpa. The Craft of Architecture" in the MAK Works on Paper Room, Saverio Anfodillo talked about his cooperation with the architect during his stay in Vienna in February 2003.

Signor Anfodillo, would you please tell us something about yourself and your work with Carlo Scarpa?
I was born the son of a Venetian family of craftsmen. My grandfather already had his own cabinetmaker business.

When was your father's company founded?
Giovanni Anfodillo & Sons was founded in 1938. The business was run by my father who also knew Carlo Scarpa.

Die Werkstatt der Firma Giovanni Anfodillo & Söhne, Venedig
Workshop of the company Giovanni Anfodillo & Sons, Venice

And where was your father's business located?
In Venice, on the Fondamenta della Sensa, near the Children's Hospital Umberto I, not far from the railroad station, in a typical quarter of craftsmen.

When did you start working for your father?
In 1950, immediately after I had finished my studies. And I also met Carlo Scarpa then. Our first cooperation was a design project concerning the Palazzo Abatellis in Palermo in the year 1953. It was a difficult commission regarding the circumstances of that time: transporting the wooden parts to Palermo on a company truck turned out a major enterprise. The roads were bad and we had a flat tire, but Carlo Scarpa wanted us to execute the details he had designed – and so we had to get the parts to Palermo.

What was the cooperation with Carlo Scarpa like?
Well, Professor Scarpa came to our workshop and explained to us what to do and which materials to use. From the very beginning, I had no doubt that he had an extraordinary understanding of our craft. He knew all materials he wanted to use. And he also knew all there was to know about wood. He sometimes even told me that he wanted to see a piece of wood used in a certain way, and when I did not completely agree with him because it was impossible to observe his suggestions he listened to reason.

The MAK has purchased Scarpa's architectural drawings made in the years of your collaboration from you. What function did these drawings have for him, and how did you use them?
I was fascinated by Scarpa's drawings, not least because he often worked freehand. His approach was just perfect – it was almost as if he were painting. And you could be sure that the first drawing would already show what he wanted. Yet, since we always discussed the projects and design problems to be solved for quite some time, he sometimes happened to do not only one, but three, four, or five drawings on the same subject. And if we had not decided to go ahead and use the newest drawing at last, Scarpa would have probably continued to develop the solution he had found in a series of drafts without end.

You once told me that Scarpa often asked you to stay longer in your workshop than usual.
He often came to see us after work. He called and asked me to hold back the workers because he would come. And when he came he insisted that the workers would stay on. And more often than not, he got what he wanted because he was so engaging and charismatic. When we tried to explain and told him, sorry, professor, but the workers do not live in Venice, they have to travel thirty kilometers to get home, he said, come on, do me a favor, we can always give them a lift. And so all of us sometimes stayed until eight or nine in the evening.

Did Scarpa consider the drawings as works of art or as means to an end? He once said that he made drawings because he wanted "to see things," and there was nothing else he could rely on.

Scarpa used the drawings only to explain what he wanted us to do. He did not consider them as works of art; he was a very humble person and did not see himself as someone doing something extraordinary – but he liked this kind of work and was a very deliberate man.

> There are many blueprints and models among the items the MAK acquired from you. What about their function?

Scarpa made drawings and was quite sure about what he was doing. Yet, he still asked us to make small wooden models to be completely on the safe side. And when he saw the finished model, he said okay, let's continue, let's set to work.

> Scarpa also asked you to build a wooden true-to-scale model, as it were, for the walling of the Tomba Brion.

The professor insisted on a fir planking to cast the walling of the Tomba Brion in concrete, literally beseeching me to use wood without any irregularities: please, Saverio, he said, the boards must be smoother than smooth. And that for the concrete casting, just imagine! I guess this incident illustrates how thorough Professor Scarpa was.

> You once said that the material, that is wood and the combination of wood and iron, was something very important to Carlo Scarpa. There was a workshop responsible for the ironworks.

The people at the forge of the Zanon company, which was only around the corner of our workshop and did all ironworks, were friends with us and with Scarpa. We always stood at the workbench together, discussing the use of materials and problems concerning the combination of wood and iron. Our collaboration was extremely fruitful because there was nobody giving orders and nobody receiving orders, we were a real team.

> Which were the most important projects Scarpa and you worked on together?

The Olivetti showroom on the Piazza San Marco, the restoration of the Galleria Querini Stampalia in Venice, the Tomba Brion. All these projects were important. Again and again, Professor Scarpa insisted on trying other materials, was not satisfied, looked for a different type of wood with specific qualities, with a certain color – and we tried to come up to his expectations. We searched all depots to find exactly the kind of wood he wanted.

> Wasn't he always looking for new materials?

Yes, and I was lucky to have good contacts with the suppliers. Time and again, we came upon new, unknown kinds of wood, and when I once told him, Professor, we have something yellow – which was what he wanted – he said that he would have a look at it as soon as he could. It was a piece of cusia [a tropical hardwood] which we had used for various doors of the Palazzo Querini Stampalia, both for exhibitions and for special details, in combination with iron. Scarpa was very happy. He said that he had finally found what he had been looking for. But he also used artificial wood besides precious woods if this complied with his ideas.

So there was a close collaboration between architect, cabinet-maker, and smith?

Yes, we three did a lot together. Well, Professor Scarpa was a very nice man though he could also be very imperious because he was always behind with his projects. Under pressure, he would send drawings with orders for immediate execution – do you understand me, Saverio, immediate!

You worked with him until his death, didn't you?

Yes, until his death. We were waiting for him to return from Japan because there was a project we were working on together, but then we got that terrible message instead.

What was your last project?

The Tomba Brion which we worked on for four or five years. That was the last project we did together.

For how long did you stay on in the workshop after Scarpa's death? You worked with your brother, didn't you?

Yes, we always worked together. We closed the workshop seven years ago, in 1996.

You mentioned that the situation had become difficult in the last years.

Very difficult. Venice is a special place, and it was impossible to rebuild the workshop in a form that would have met the new requirements. Since we had neither enough room nor the possibility to install facilities for removing fumes and refuse, we had only two options: to move or to close it. Finally, we decided to close the workshop because we had also reached a certain age and our sons had not followed us. This is why we said, okay, that's the end of it.

The conversation with Saverio Anfodillo was conducted by MAK curator Rainald Franz

Your collaboration with Carlo Scarpa lasted for at least thirty years.

Yes, for more than thirty years.

Was it something special to work with him? And if so, what was so unusual about it?

It was his verve. He was friendly, he had a feeling for the craft, and he appreciated our work. He was always kind to us and never asked us to do anything we couldn't.

Was working with him fun or rather something that yielded a considerable profit?

To tell you the truth: I learnt a lot and I had a lot of fun working with Professor Scarpa but there was certainly no money in his commissions. We often had to do something twice or even thrice until the piece was as perfect as he wanted it.

Would such a collaboration still be possible today?

No, it's a pity but I don't think so. All our crafts will soon be extinct. Today's architects have a different approach. Their drafts are finished, and they just want to see them executed. Nowadays, craftsmen are forced to close their workshops because manual work has become unaffordable due to the cost of labor and the strict legal conditions. Everything is mass-produced these days, which was something Professor Scarpa did not care for. His things were unique.

Biografie Biography

Carlo Scarpa wird am 2. Juni 1906 in Venedig geboren.
Carlo Scarpa is born in Venice on June 2, 1906.

1926 Diplom der Kunstgewerbeschule, Venedig; Assistent am Institut für Architektur der Universität Venedig (Istituto Universitario di Architettura di Venezia, IUAV) bei Prof. Guido Cirili
Venice Arts and Crafts College diploma; assistant lecturer at the Venice University Institute of Architecture (Istituto Universitario di Architettura di Venezia, IUAV) with Prof. Guido Cirili

Ab 1933 Zusammenarbeit mit der Firma Venini auf Murano, Glasentwürfe
From 1933 on Collaboration with the Venini company, Murano, glassware designs

1952 Freie Dozentur für Innenarchitektur am IUAV
Free lecturer for interior design at the IUAV

1955 Ernennung zum Doktor honoris causa
Honorary doctorate

1967 Reise nach Amerika zur Gestaltung des italienischen Pavillons der Expo Montreal. Besuch der Schule Frank Lloyd Wrights in Taliesin/Arizona; Bekanntschaft mit Louis Kahn
Journey to America: commission to design the Italian pavilion at the Montreal Expo. Visits Frank Lloyd Wright's school in Taliesin, Arizona; meets Louis Kahn

1972 Ernennung zum Rektor des IUAV
Director of the IUAV

1976 Ende der Lehrtätigkeit an der Universität
Stops teaching at the university

Am 28. November 1978 stirbt Carlo Scarpa an den Folgen eines Unfalls in Sendai, Japan.
Carlo Scarpa dies as a result of an accident in Sendai, Japan, on November 28, 1978.

Carlo Scarpa am Zeichentisch
Carlo Scarpa at a drawing board

Ausgewählte Projekte
Selected Projects

1928
Kristalllustergeschäft für Cappellin & Co., Lungarno Gucciardini, Florenz
Crystal chandelier shop for Cappellin & Co., Lungarno Gucciardini, Florence

1931
Wohnung Ferruccio Asta, Venedig
Ferruccio Asta Flat, Venice

1932
Beteiligung am Wettbewerb für die neue Ponte dell'Accademia, Venedig
Contribution to a competition concerning the new Ponte dell'Accademia, Venice

1934
Wettbewerbsbeiträge für eine städtebauliche Planung Mestres (mit de Luigi) und einen Flughafen auf dem Lido von Venedig (mit Pelizzari und Piamonte)
Contributions to competitions concerning an urban plan for Mestre (with de Luigi) and an airport on the Lido of Venice (with Pelizzari and Piamonte)

1935
Entwurf für die Wohnung Bassani, Cortina d'Ampezzo (nicht realisiert)
Design for Bassani Flat, Cortina d'Ampezzo (not realized)

1936/37
Restaurierung der Innenräume der Ca' Foscari, Venedig (Adaptierung für die Wirtschafts- und Handelsfakultät der Universität Venedig)
Restoration of the interior of the Ca' Foscari, Venice (adaptation for the Venice University Department of Economics and Trade)

1937
Gestaltung der Ausstellung „Oreficeria Veneziana" [„Venezianische Goldschmiedekunst"], Loggetta del Sansovino, Venedig
Design of the exhibition "Oreficeria Veneziana" ["The Art of Venetian Goldsmiths"], Loggetta del Sansovino, Venice

1941
Entwurf Familiengrab Rizzo, Friedhofsinsel San Michele, Venedig (nicht realisiert)
Restaurierung des Hauses Sacerdoti, Venedig
Innenraumgestaltung der Wohnung Arturo Martini, Venedig
Design of the Rizzo family tomb, San Michele cemetery island, Venice (not realized)
Restoration of Sacerdoti House, Venice
Interior design of Arturo Martini Flat, Venice

1942
Gestaltung der Galerie „Il Cavallino", Venedig
Design of the Gallery "Il Cavallino," Venice

1946
Entwurf eines Kinos für Valdobbiadene
Design of a cinema for Valdobbiadene

1946–52
Umgestaltung der Räume in der Galleria dell'Accademia, Venedig
Redesign of the rooms of the Galleria dell'Accademia, Venice

1947–50
Haus Giacomuzzi, Udine
Giacomuzzi House, Udine

1948
Gestaltung der Ausstellung „Paul Klee" für die XXIV. Biennale, Venedig
Entwurf für eine Kirche aus vorgefertigten Bauteilen, Torre di Mosto (nicht realisiert)
Design of exhibition "Paul Klee" for the XXIV Venice Biennial
Design of a church made of prefabricated parts, Torre di Mosto (not realized)

1948/49
Kino „Astra", San Donà di Piave
Entwurf für ein Wohnhaus in Feltre (nicht realisiert)
Cinema "Astra," San Donà di Piave
Design of a residential building for Feltre (not realized)

1950
Entwurf Haus Bortolotto, Cervignano (nicht realisiert)
Villa Guarnieri, Lido di Venezia, Venedig
Einrichtung des italienischen Pavillons für die XXV. Biennale, Venedig
Gestaltung von Buchhandlung und Antiquariat Ferdinando Ongania, Venedig
Design of Bortolotto House, Cervignano (not realized)
Villa Guarnieri, Lido di Venezia, Venice
Furnishings for Italian pavilion at the XXV Venice Biennial
Design of bookshop and antiquarian bookshop Ferdinando Ongania, Venice

1951
Gestaltung der Ausstellung „Giovanni Battista Tiepolo", Venedig
Design of the exhibition "Giovanni Battista Tiepolo," Venice

1952
Gestaltung der italienischen Halle für die XXVI. Biennale, Venedig
Gestaltung der Ausstellung „La grafica di Henri de Toulouse-Lautrec" [„Die Grafik Henri de Toulouse-Lautrecs"], Museo Correr, Aula Napoleonica, Venedig
Design of Italian hall for the XXVI Venice Biennial
Design of the exhibition "La grafica di Henri de Toulouse-Lautrec" ["Henri de Toulouse-Lautrec – The Graphic Work"], Aula Napoleonica, Venice

1953
Entwurf Villa Zoppas, Conegliano (nicht realisiert)
Design for Villa Zoppas, Conegliano (not realized)

Ab 1953 From 1953 on
Adaptierung und Umgestaltung des Museo Correr, Venedig
Adaptation and redesign of the Museo Correr, Venice

1953/54
Neugestaltung und Adaptierung des Palazzo Abatellis, Palermo, als Galleria nazionale di Sicilia*
Neubau des Pavillons für Venezuela für die XXVII. Biennale, Venedig*
Refurbishment and reorganization of the Palazzo Abatellis, Palermo, as the Galleria nazionale di Sicilia*
Reconstruction of the Venezuelan pavilion at the XXVII Venice Biennial*

1954
Gestaltung der Ausstellung „Arte antica cinese" [„Antike chinesische Kunst"], Palazzo Ducale (Dogenpalast), Venedig*
Design of exhibition "Arte antica cinese" ["Ancient Chinese Art"], Palazzo Ducale, Venice*

1955
Aula Tribunale (Schwurgerichtssaal) „Manlio Capitolo", Venedig*
Aula Tribunale (jury courtroom) "Manlio Capitolo," Venice*

1955/56
Umgestaltung von Sälen in der Galleria degli Uffizi, Florenz (mit Gardella und Michelucci)
Restaurierung und Neugestaltung der Aula Magna di Ca' Foscari, Universität Venedig*
Refurbishment of various halls of the Galleria degli Uffizi, Florence (with Gardella and Michelucci)
Restoration and redesign of the Aula Magna di Ca' Foscari, Venice University*

1955–57
Zubau zur Gipsoteca Canoviana, Possagno*
Extension of the Gipsoteca Canoviana, Possagno*

1955–61
Villa Veritti, Udine

1956
Gestaltung der Ausstellung „Piet Mondrian", Galleria Nazionale in der Villa Giulia, Rom
Wettbewerbsbeitrag für die Colonia Olivetti, Ivrea (mit D'Agaro, Detti, Pastor)
Design of exhibition "Piet Mondrian," Galleria Nazionale in the Villa Giulia, Rome
Contribution to the competition concerning the Colonia Olivetti, Ivrea (with D'Agaro, Detti, Pastor)

1956–73
Umgestaltung des Museo di Castelvecchio, Verona*
Redesign of the Museo di Castelvecchio, Verona*

1957
Campingplatz „Malcontenta", Fusina bei Venedig*
Camping site "Malcontenta", Fusina near Venice*

1957/58
Olivetti-Schauraum, Markusplatz, Venedig*
Olivetti showroom, Piazza San Marco, Venice*

1958
Gestaltung des italienischen Pavillons für die XXIX. Biennale, Venedig
Gestaltung der Ausstellung „Vetri di Murano" [„Muranoglas"], Venedig
Design of the Italian pavilion at the XXIX Venice Biennial
Design of the exhibition "Vetri di Murano" ["Glasses of Murano"], Venice

1959
Gestaltung der Ausstellung „Un secolo d'arte del vetro a Murano" [„Ein Jahrhundert Glaskunst aus Murano"], Palazzo della Gran Guardia, Verona
Design of the exhibition "Un secolo d'arte del vetro a Murano" ["One Hundred Years of Glass Art on Murano"], Palazzo della Gran Guardia, Verona

1960
Adaptierung des zweiten Stockwerks des Museo Correr (Quadreria), Venedig*
Gestaltung der Ausstellung „Il disegni di Erich Mendelsohn" [„Die Zeichnungen Erich Mendelsohns"] für die XXX. Biennale, Venedig
Adaption of the second floor of the Museo Correr (Quadreria), Venice*
Design of exhibition "Il disegni di Erich Mendelsohn" ["The Drawings of Erich Mendelsohn"] at the XXX Venice Biennial

1961–63
Gavina-Schauraum, Via Altabella, Bologna
Erdgeschoss, Ausstellungsräume und Garten des Palazzo Querini Stampalia, Venedig*
Umbau und Erweiterung des Hauses Zentner, Zürich*
Gavina showroom, Via Altabella, Bologna
Ground floor, exhibition rooms, and courtyard of the Palazzo Querini Stampalia, Venice*
Conversion and extension of the Zentner House, Zurich*

1963
Haus Cassina, Ronco di Carimate
Innenraumgestaltung des Museums Revoltella, Triest
Planung für den Wiederaufbau des Teatro Carlo Felice, Genua
Cassina House, Ronco di Carimate
Interior design of the Museo Revoltella, Trieste
Plan for the reconstruction of the Teatro Carlo Felice, Genoa

1966
Teilnahme am internationalen Wettbewerb für die Neue Pinakothek, München
Gestaltung der Biennale-Ausstellung „Aspetti del primo astrattismo italiano, Milano – Como 1930–1940" [„Aspekte früher abstrakter Malerei in Italien, Mailand – Como 1930–1940"] mit Werken von Lucio Fontana, Alberto Viani und Giorgio Morandi
Gestaltung der Ausstellung „Museum Architecture", Museum of Modern Art, New York
Participation in the international competition concerning the Neue Pinakothek, Munich
Design of the Biennial exhibition "Aspetti del primo astrattismo italiano, Milano – Como 1930–1940" ["Aspects of Early Abstract Painting in Italy, Milan – Como 1930–1940"] with works by Lucio Fontana, Alberto Viani, and Giorgio Morandi
Design of the exhibition "Museum Architecture," Museum of Modern Art, New York

1967
Gestaltung der Ausstellung „La Poesia" [„Die Poesie"] im italienischen Pavilon, Expo '67, Montreal, Kanada
Design of the exhibition "La Poesia" ["Poetry"] in the Italian pavilion, Montreal Expo '67, Canada

1968
Design für den Tisch „Doge" für Gavina
Gestaltung der Ausstellung „Linee della ricerca contemporanea: dall' informale alle nuove strutture" [„Linien moderner Suche: Vom Informel zu neuen Strukturen"] mit Werken von Francesco Albini, Louis Kahn, Pavel Rudolf und Carlo Scarpa für die XXXIV. Biennale, Venedig
Design of "Doge" table for Gavina
Design of the exhibition "Linee della ricerca contemporanea: dall' informale alle nuove strutture" ["Lines of Modern Search – From Art Informel to New Structures"] at the XXXIV Venice Biennial with works by Francesco Albini, Louis Kahn, Pavel Rudolf, and Carlo Scarpa

1969
Gestaltung der Ausstellung „Frescoes from Florence" [„Fresken aus Florenz"], Hayward Gallery, London
Gestaltung der Ausstellung „Erich Mendelsohn. Drawings" [„Erich Mendelsohn. Zeichnungen"], University of California, Berkeley
Design of the exhibition "Frescoes from Florence," Hayward Gallery, London
Design of the exhibition "Erich Mendelsohn. Drawings," University of California, Berkeley

1970
Castello di Brescia, Brescia, Umbau zum Waffenmuseum (realisiert 1973)*
Gestaltung der Ausstellung „Giorgio Morandi", Royal Academy of Fine Arts, London
Haus Masieri, Venedig
Castello di Brescia, Brescia, conversion into a museum of ancient weapons (realized in 1973)*
Design of the exhibition "Giorgio Morandi," Royal Academy of Fine Arts, London
Masieri House, Venice

1970–78
Tomba Brion (Familiengrab der Familie Brion), San Vito d'Altivole*
Tomba Brion (Brion family tomb), San Vito d'Altivole*

1971
Teilnahme an der Ausstellung „Important Drawings of Architecture" [„Wichtige Architekturzeichnungen"], Heinz Gallery, London
Participation in the exhibition "Important Drawings of Architecture," Heinz Gallery, London

1972
Instandsetzung des Teatro Carlo Felice, Genua
Renovation of the Teatro Carlo Felice, Genoa

1973
Entwurf für das Museum Villa Strozzi, Florenz (nicht realisiert)
Design for the Museum Villa Strozzi, Florence (not realized)

1973–81
Erweiterung und Umgestaltung der Banca Popolare di Verona, Verona
Extension and reorganization of the Banca Popolare di Verona, Verona

1974
Entwurf für das Nationalmuseum Messina (nicht realisiert)
Außengestaltung der Villa Il Palazzetto, Monselice*
Gestaltung der Ausstellung „Venezia e Bisanzio" [„Venedig und Byzanz"], Palazzo Ducale (Dogenpalast), Venedig*
Design for the National Museum Messina (not realized)
Exterior design of the Villa Il Palazzetto, Monselice*
Design of the exhibition "Venezia e Bisanzio" ["Venice and Byzantium"], Palazzo Ducale, Venice*

1974/75
Instandsetzung des Klosters Santa Caterina im Museo Civico, Treviso
Renovation of the Santa Caterina Monastery at the Museo Civico, Treviso

1975
Denkmal für die Gefallenen, Piazza della Loggia, Brescia*
Haus Ottolenghi, Bardolino
Instandsetzung des Auditorium Maximum des IUAV (Istituto Universitario di Architettura di Venezia), Venedig
Monument for the war dead, Piazza della Loggia, Brescia*
Ottolenghi House, Bardolino
Renovation of the main auditorium of the IUAV (Istituto Universitario di Architettura di Venezia), Venice

1975–78
Wiederaufbau und Erweiterung des Klosters San Sebastiano, Fakultät für Philosophie und Literatur, Universität Venedig*
Reconstruction and extension of the San Sebastiano Monastery, Venice University, Department of Philosophy and Literature*

1976
Entwurf für einen Umbau des Musée Picasso, Paris (nicht realisiert)
Plan for a reorganization of the Musée Picasso, Paris (not realized)

1977
Neugestaltung des Eingangs zum IUAV, Venedig
Redesign of the entrance to the IUAV, Venice

1978
Entwurf für eine Wohnhausanlage in Riad, Saudi-Arabien
Projekt für eine Filiale der Banca Popolare di Verona in Gemona
Design of a residential complex in Riyadh, Saudi Arabia
Project for a branch of the Banca Popolare di Verona in Gemona

* gemeinsam mit der Kunsttischlerei Giovanni Anfodillo & Söhne
* in co-operation with the cabinetmakers Giovanni Anfodillo & Sons

Ausgewählte Bibliografie
Selected Bibliography

P. Duboy: „Locus Solus. Carlo Scarpa et le cimitére de San Vito d'Altivole (1969–1975)", in: *L'Architecture d'Aujourd'hui*, 181/1975, S. pp. 73–86

C. Scarpa: Memoriae Causa, Verona 1977

C. Scarpa: „Volevo ritagliare l'azzurro del cielo", in: *Rassegna,* 7/1981, S. pp. 82–84

A. Rudi: „Carlo Scarpa, Frammenti 1926–1978", in: *Rassegna,* 7/1981, S. pp. 44–53, 70–76

Carlo Scarpa a Castelvecchio, hg. von ed. by L. Magagnato, Mailand Milan, Ausstellungskatalog exhibition catalogue Museo di Castelvecchio, 1982

F. Dal Co/G. Mazzariol: Carlo Scarpa. Opera Completa, Mailand Milan 1984

M. A. Crippa: Carlo Scarpa. Il pensiero, il disegno, i progetti, Mailand Milan 1984

Carlo Scarpa. Il progetto per Santa Caterina a Treviso, Ausstellungskatalog exhibition catalogue Treviso 1984

F. Fonatti: Elemente des Bauens bei Carlo Scarpa, Wien Vienna 1985

V. Magnago Lampugnani: Carlo Scarpa. Architektur, Stuttgart 1986

A. F. Marcianò: Carlo Scarpa, Zürich Zurich 1986

M. Frascari: The Body and Architecture in the Drawings of Carlo Scarpa, Cambridge, Mass. 1987

C. Hoh-Slodczyk: Carlo Scarpa und das Museum, Berlin 1987

B. Albertini: Scarpa. L'architettura nel dettaglio, Rom Rome 1988

Carlo Scarpa. Die andere Stadt The Other City, hg. von ed. by P. Noever/P. Duboy, Ausstellungskatalog exhibition catalogue MAK, Wien Vienna 1989

R. Murphy: Carlo Scarpa & Castelvecchio, Venedig Venice 1991

S. Polano: Carlo Scarpa a Palazzo Abatellis. L'allestimento della Galleria Nazionale di Sicilia, 1953–54, Mailand Milan 1991

B. Albertini: Scarpa. Musei e esposizioni, Mailand Milan 1992

R. Murphy: Querini Stampalia Foundation, London 1993

S. Los: Carlo Scarpa, Köln Cologne 1994

M. A. Stern: „Passage in the Garden: An Iconology of the Brion Tomb", in: *Landscape Journal,* 1994, S. pp. 39–57

D. Hezel: Architekten – Carlo Scarpa. IRB-Literaturauslese 1350, Stuttgart 1995

S. Los: Carlo Scarpa. Guida all'architettura, Venedig Venice 1995 (English edition: Carlo Scarpa. An Architectural Guide, Venice 1995)

M. Mazza: Carlo Scarpa alla Querini Stampalia: Disegni inediti, Venedig Venice 1996

F. Dal Co: Villa Ottolenghi. Carlo Scarpa, New York 1998

Carlo Scarpa, Architect Interventing with History, Ausstellungskatalog exhibition catalogue Canadian Centre for Architecture (CCA), Montréal 1999

R. Franz: „Raum und Zeichnung im Werk von Carlo Scarpa", in: 2MAK. Räume/Spaces, The MAK Backstage Book 2001, Wien–Los Angeles Vienna–Los Angeles 1999, S. pp. 45–53

Carlo Scarpa. Mostre e Musei 1944–1976. Case e Paesaggi 1972–1978, Ausstellungskatalog exhibition catalogue Museo di Castelvecchio, Verona/Palazzo Barbaran da Porto, Vincenza 2000

Zeichnungen, Planpausen und Modelle im Bestand des MAK,
erworben aus dem Besitz der Firma Giovanni Anfodillo & Söhne, Venedig

**Drawings, blueprints, and models owned by the MAK,
purchased from the company Giovanni Anfodillo & Sons, Venice**

Campingplatz Camping site „Malcontenta", Fusina bei Venedig Fusina near Venice
Entwurf der Türgriffe und Beschläge mit der Gesamttür Design of door handles and fittings with entire door, 1957
Pause auf Velin Blueprint on vellum paper
59 x 109,5 cm
Inv.-Nr. K.I. 15154/1

Campingplatz Camping site „Malcontenta", Fusina bei Venedig Fusina near Venice
Entwurf der Türgriffe und Beschläge mit der Gesamttür Design of door handles and fittings with entire door, 1957
Entwurfspapier, Bleistift, roter, gelber Buntstift Sketching paper, pencil, red, yellow crayon
29,5 x 106 cm
Inv.-Nr. K.I. 15154/1/2

Campingplatz Camping site „Malcontenta", Fusina bei Venedig Fusina near Venice
Details der Türen Door details, 1957
Entwurfspapier, Bleistift Sketching paper, pencil
29,5 x 113 cm
Inv.-Nr. K.I. 15154/1/3

Entwurf für eine Anrichte Design of a sideboard
Mit drei Kompartimenten im Unterteil, auf Stehern, in Metall und Douglasie, auf der Rückseite zwei Köpfe, der eine ein Selbstporträt Carlo Scarpas, o. J. With three compartments in the lower part, on posts, metal and Douglas fir, verso two heads, one of them a self-portrait of Carlo Scarpa, undated
Steifpapier, Bleistift Stiffening paper, pencil
22,5 x 63 cm
Inv.-Nr. K.I. 15154/2*, 15154/3

Gelände der Biennale Venedig Venice Biennial premises, Giardini
Eingang und Gartenhof, Stufen Portal and garden patio, stairs, 1952
Entwurfspapier, Bleistift, Kohle Sketching paper, pencil, charcoal
29,5 x 52 cm
Inv.-Nr. K.I. 15154/4

Gelände der Biennale Venedig Venice Biennial premises, Giardini
Eingang und Gartenhof, Rahmenverbindung im Querschnitt, o.J. Portal and garden patio, section of framework connection, undated
Entwurfspapier, Bleistift, signiert Sketching paper, pencil, signed
25 x 18 cm
Inv.-Nr. K.I. 15154/5

Gelände der Biennale Venedig Venice Biennial premises, Giardini
Perspektive zu den Stiegen, Gartenhof, Querschnitt und Festlegung der Stufenabfolge Perspective of stairs, garden patio, section and arrangement of stairs, 1952
Entwurfspapier, Bleistift Sketching paper, pencil
30 x 48 cm
Inv.-Nr. K.I. 15154/6*

Detail eines Rundstabs aus drei Teilen für einen Handlauf Detail of a three-part pole for a handrail
Querschnitt und Aufsicht des Profils, o. J. Section and top view of the profile, undated
Entwurfspapier Sketching paper
22 x 33 cm
Inv.-Nr. K.I. 15154/7–9

Serie von 12 Entwürfen für die Biennale Venedig bzw. das Museo Correr, Venedig Series of 12 designs for the Venice Biennial or the Museo Correr, Venice, 1952/53
Entwurfspapier, Kopien auf Papier Sketching paper, copies on paper
Je Each 35,5 x 30 cm
Inv.-Nr. K.I. 15154/10/1–12

Museo di Castelvecchio, Verona
Skizze für die Besucherbänke Sketch of the visitor benches, 1956–64
Bleistift auf Papier, auf der Rückseite auch roter Buntstift Pencil on paper, verso also with red crayon
31,5 x 43 cm
Inv.-Nr. K.I. 15154/11* Seite Page 61

Museo di Castelvecchio, Verona
2 Blatt Entwürfe für Besucherbänke in Holz 2 sheets with designs for wooden visitor benches, 1956–64
Bleistift, roter Buntstift auf Papier, doppelseitig angelegt Pencil, red crayon on paper, recto and verso
Je Each 22 x 29 cm
Inv.-Nr. K.I. 15154/12/1, 2

Museo di Castelvecchio, Verona
Gitter, Muster Grille model, 1956–64
Bleistift, Buntstift, Filzstift in Rot und Blau auf einem Brief der Architekturfakultät der Universität Venedig und auf Papier Pencil, crayon, felt tip in red and blue on a letter of the Architectural Department of the University of Venice and on paper
Je Each 28,5 x 21 cm
Inv.-Nr. K.I. 15154/13/1, 2

Museo di Castelvecchio, Verona
Perspektive der Bank mit handschriftlichen Materialangaben (Plastik, Palisanderholz) von Carlo Scarpa Perspective of the bench with handwritten details concerning the materials (plastic, rosewood) by Carlo Scarpa, 1956–64
Entwurfspapier, Bleistift, Buntstift Sketching paper, pencil, crayon
37 x 120 cm
Inv.-Nr. K.I. 15154/14*

Museo di Castelvecchio, Verona
Aufriss, farbig angelegt, Details Elevation, colored, details, 1956–64
Dünner Karton, Bleistift, Kugelschreiber, roter und gelber Buntstift, roter Filzstift Thin cardboard, pencil, ballpoint, red, yellow crayon, red felt tip
70 x 100 cm
Inv.-Nr. K.I. 15154/15*

Wohnung Sign. Carrain Flat Sign. Carrain, Padua
Grundriss, Aufriss des Betts und der Schrankfronten (5 Perspektiven), o. J. Floor plan, elevation of bed and wardrobe fronts (5 perspectives), undated
Planpause, übergangen mit Bleistift, blauer, roter, gelber Buntstift, Kugelschreiber, Bleistiftzeichnung auf der Rückseite Blueprint, pencil revisions, blue, red, yellow crayon, ballpoint, verso pencil drawing
108 x 71 cm
Inv.-Nr. K.I. 15154/16/1

Wohnung Sign. Carrain Flat Sign. Carrain, Padua
Aufriss, Perspektive der Innengestaltung des Kleiderschrankes, Details der Gestaltung, o. J. Elevation, perspective of wardrobe interior, details of design, undated
Planpause, übergangen mit Bleistift, rotem, grünem, blauem Buntstift Blueprint, pencil revisions, red, green, blue crayon
108 x 71 cm
Inv.-Nr. K.I. 15154/16/2

Ausstellungsschrank für die Triennale di Milano Showcase for the Triennale di Milano
Grundriss und Sockeldetails, o. J. Outline and base details, undated
Planpause, mit Bleistiftspuren am Rand Blueprint, edges with pencil traces
74 x 104 cm
Inv.-Nr. K.I. 15154/17

Olivetti-Schauraum, Venedig Olivetti showroom, Venice
Perspektive und Aufriss der Wandkonsole mit Materialangabe und Facheinteilung Perspective and elevation of wall console with details concerning the material and the division of the shelves, 1957–58
Entwurfspapier, grüner, violetter Buntstift, Bleistift Sketching paper, green, violet crayon, pencil
29 x 67 cm
Inv.-Nr. K.I. 15154/18

Servierwagen für einen Privatkunden Trolley for a private client
Planpause mit Details des Aufbaus, Materialangaben, o. J. Blue print with details of the structure, specifications regarding the material, undated
43 x 95 cm
Inv.-Nr. K.I. 15154/19*

Rahmenentwürfe für Leinwände Frame designs for canvases
Zeichnung der Umrisse und Profile der Rahmen, o. J. Outline drawings and frame profiles, undated
Entwurfspapier, Bleistift Sketching paper, pencil
Je Each 35 x 50 cm
Inv.-Nr. K.I. 15154/20, 15154/21

Tisch für Luigi Nono Table for Luigi Nono
Details der Winkel und der Verschraubung, o. J. Details of angles and screws, undated
Entwurfspapier, Bleistift Sketching paper, pencil
30 x 39 cm
Inv.-Nr. K.I. 15154/22*   Seite Page 21

Haus Zentner, Zürich Zentner House, Zurich
Heizkörperabdeckung der Nische im Speisesaal, mit Material- und Maßangaben, 2 Querschnitte Radiator cover for the dining room recess, with details concerning the material and measurements, 2 sections, 1961–66
Planpause, mit Bleistift überzeichnet Blueprint, pencil revisions
45,5 x 100 cm
Inv.-Nr. K.I. 15154/23*   Seite Page 31 oben top

Haus Zentner, Zürich Zentner House, Zurich
Querschnitte und Perspektiven der Halterungen Sections and perspectives of the fixtures, 1961–66
Karton, Bleistift, gelber, blauer, orange Buntstift Cardboard, pencil, yellow, blue, orange crayon
50 x 70 cm
Inv.-Nr. K.I. 15154/24*   Seite Page 29

Haus Zentner, Zürich Zentner House, Zurich
Handlauf für eine Treppe, Skizze, doppelseitig bezeichnet Handrail for a stairway, draft, recto and verso, 1961–66
Entwurfspapier, Bleistift Sketching paper, pencil
30 x 47 cm
Inv.-Nr. K.I. 15154/25/1

Haus Zentner, Zürich Zentner House, Zurich
Detail, Maßangaben Detail, measurements, 1961–66
Papier, Tusche, Bleistift Paper, ink, pencil
22 x 31 cm
Inv.-Nr. K.I. 15154/25/2

Zeltkonstruktion für Nini Scarpa Tent structure for Nini Scarpa
Gelenks- und Ständerkonstruktion für ein Zelt, Querschnitt und Maße der Träger und Gelenke mit Details der Verbindungen, o. J. Joint and pole construction, section and measurements of supporting beams and joints with details of connections, undated
Entwurfspapier, Bleistift Sketching paper, pencil
44 x 120 cm
Inv.-Nr. K.I. 15154/26

Schreibmöbel für Nini Scarpa Desk for Nini Scarpa
Entwurfszeichnung mit Details und Querschnitten der Trägerkonstruktion mit Angaben des Materials und der Maße, o. J. Draft with details and sections of the supporting construction with specifications concerning the material and measurements, undated
Entwurfspapier, blauer, grüner Filzstift Sketching paper, blue, green felt tip
30 x 52 cm
Inv.-Nr. K.I. 15154/27*   Seite Page 20

Gitter für eine Tür Door grille
Aufriss und Querschnitt mit Materialangaben, o. J. Elevation and section with details concerning the material, undated
Entwurfskarton, Bleistift, roter Buntstift Cardboard, pencil, red crayon
47,5 x 75 cm
Inv.-Nr. K.I. 15154/28

Küchenmöbel mit Klapptür Cupboard with trapdoor
Planpause mit händischen Eintragungen Carlo Scarpas, Kugelschreiberzeichnung auf der Rückseite, o. J. Blueprint on paper with handwritten pencil notes by Carlo Scarpa, ballpoint drawing on verso, undated
Planpause auf Papier, Bleistift, Kugelschreiber Blueprint on paper, pencil, ballpoint
65 x 47,5 cm
Inv.-Nr. K.I. 15154/29

Bibliothek mit Porträt von Tobia Scarpa Library with portrait of Tobia Scarpa
Doppelseitiger Entwurf für Bücherregale und Ladenelemente mit Angabe des Materials, Zeichnung von Tobia Scarpa als „Modulor", o. J. Designs of shelves and drawers with material specifications on recto and verso, portrait of Tobia Scarpa as "modulor", undated
Entwurfskarton, Bleistift, Kugelschreiber Cardboard, pencil, ballpoint
35 x 100 cm
Inv.-Nr. K.I. 15154/30*   Seite Page 22

Wendeltreppe für das Haus Muraro, Venedig Spiral staircase for the Muraro House, Venice
Aufsicht der Spindel mit Angaben zu den Maßen, Maßstab 1:5, doppelseitig bezeichnet Top view of newel with details concerning measurements, scale 1:5, drawings on recto and verso, 1975
Entwurfskarton, Bleistift, roter, blauer, gelber, orange Buntstift, verso nur Bleistift Cardboard, pencil, red, blue, yellow, orange crayon, only pencil on verso
35 x 49,5 cm
Inv.-Nr. K.I. 15154/31/1*   Seite Page 24

Wendeltreppe für das Haus Muraro, Venedig Spiral staircase for the Muraro House, Venice
Aufsicht des Ständers und der ansetzenden Stufe mit Details der Konstruktion, Maßen und Materialangaben Top view of post and first step with construction details, measurements, and material specifications, 1975
Planpause mit Korrekturen in Bleistift, gelbem Buntstift Blueprint with pencil and yellow crayon revisions
60,2 x 97,5 cm
Inv.-Nr. K.I. 15154/31/2*   Seite Page 25

Wandablauf mit drei Türen Wall sequence with three doors
Aufriss der Wand mit Angaben zur Konstruktion der Türen und des Gangs davor mit Maßangaben, Maßstab 1:20, o. J. Elevation of wall with details concerning the construction of the doors and the corridor in front of it, with measurements, scale 1:20, undated
Planpause mit Korrekturen in Bleistift, Kugelschreiber Blueprint with pencil and ballpoint revisions
59 x 70 cm
Inv.-Nr. K.I. 15154/32

Waffenmuseum Museum of Ancient Weapons Castello di Brescia, Brescia
Detailzeichnung der Glieder des Treppengeländers Detail drawing of banister elements, 1971
Entwurfspapier, Bleistift, roter, blauer, grüner, gelber Buntstift Sketching paper, pencil, red, blue, green, yellow pencil
32,5 x 45 cm
Inv.-Nr. K.I. 15154/33* Seite Page 58

Villa Il Palazzetto, Monselice
Details der beiden Türen in Holz und Glas, die die Drehtür bilden, in Originalgröße, handschriftliche Angaben von Carlo Scarpa, 2 Vertikalschnitte der symmetrisch gedachten Türen, Januar 1974 Details of the two doors in wood and glass forming the revolving door in their original dimensions, handwritten notes by Carlo Scarpa, 2 vertical sections of the symmetric doors, January 1974
Planpause mit Überzeichnung, Bleistift, roter, gelber, blauer Buntstift Drawing on blueprint, pencil, red, yellow, blue crayon
44,5 x 87,1 cm
Inv.-Nr. K.I. 15154/34* Seite Page 37 unten bottom

Holzgelenke Wooden joints
Mit handschriftlichen Vermerken zum Material und zu den Maßen, o. J. With handwritten material specifications and details concerning the measurements, undated
Planpause Blueprint
32 x 64 cm
Inv.-Nr. K.I. 15154/35*

Villa Il Palazzetto, Monselice
Entwürfe für die Tür- und Fensterschließer, Februar 1974/Mai 1974 Designs of door and window catches, February 1974/May 1974
Planpause, Bleistift, roter, blauer Buntstift Blueprint, pencil, red, blue crayon
30 x 65 cm
Inv.-Nr. K.I. 15154/36* Seite Page 37 oben top

Villa Il Palazzetto, Monselice
Details in Originalgröße für die beiden Türen in Holz/Thermopan-Glas Details of the two doors in wood and Thermopane in their original dimensions, 1974
Planpause, mit Bleistift, rotem, gelbem Buntstift überzeichnet Drawing on blueprint, pencil, red, yellow crayon
48,5 x 97,2 cm
Inv.-Nr. K.I. 15154/37

Villa Il Palazzetto, Monselice
Aufrisse und Grundriss sowie Details und Maßangaben der Beschläge der Tür des Hintereingangs, Jänner 1974/Mai 1974 Elevations and ground plans including details and measurements of the fittings for the rear door, January 1974, May 1974
Planpause mit Korrekturen in Bleistift, rotem Buntstift Blueprint with pencil and red crayon revisions
75,5 x 40,2 cm
Inv.-Nr. K.I. 15154/38

Villa Il Palazzetto, Monselice
Detailzeichnung der Türen und Fenster mit Beschlägen, in Querschnitt und Aufsicht, 13. Mai 1974 Detail drawing of doors and windows with fittings, cross-section and top view, May 13, 1974
Planpause mit Korrekturen mit Bleistift, rotem, gelbem Buntstift Blueprint with revisions (pencil, red, yellow crayon)
76 x 26 cm
Inv.-Nr. K.I. 15154/39* Seite Page 36

Vorhangstange Curtain rod
Querschnitt und Detailzeichnung in Originalgröße im Verhältnis zum ebenfalls angelegten Fensterrahmen, o. J. Cross-section and detail drawing of the rod in its original dimension in relation to the also depicted window frame, undated
2 Kartonteile, Entwurfspapier, mit Klebeband zusammengefügt, collagiert, Bleistift, gelber, roter Buntstift 2 cardboard parts, sketching paper, joined with adhesive tape, collaged, pencil, yellow, red crayon
60 x 52 cm
Inv.-Nr. K.I. 15154/40* Seite Page 32

Bücherregal für die Schwägerin Carlo Scarpas Bookshelf for Carlo Scarpa's sister-in-law
Perspektive und Front des Regals mit Detailskizzen und Materialangaben, o. J. Perspective and front of shelf with detail sketches and material specifications, undated
Karton, Bleistift, Tinte, roter Buntstift Cardboard, pencil, ink, red crayon
49,5 x 35 cm
Inv.-Nr. K.I. 15154/41/1* Seite Page 23

Bibliothek für die Schwägerin Carlo Scarpas Library for Carlo Scarpa's sister-in-law
Doppelseitige Skizze mit Möbelteilen und Regalen, Maßstab 1:25, o. J. Double-page sketch with furniture elements and shelves, scale 1:25, undated
Blockpapier mit Perforation am oberen Rand, Bleistift, grüner Filzstift (recto und verso), gelber Buntstift Pad paper with perforation along the upper edge, pencil, green felt tip (on recto and verso), yellow crayon
32 x 22 cm
Inv.-Nr. K.I. 15154/41/2*

Tomba Brion, San Vito d'Altivole
Detail der Rundstäbe für die Sakristei der Tomba Brion, Querschnitte Detail of round bars for the vestry, cross-sections, 1970–1978
Entwurfspapier, Bleistift, blaue Tinte Sketching paper, pencil, blue ink
29,7 x 29,7 cm
Inv.-Nr. K.I. 15154/42

Piazza della Loggia, Brescia
Abspannung vor einer Säule, Maßstab 1:10, unten Skizze eines Objekts, Hand und Kubus, Entwurf für ein Denkmal Anchoring in front of a column, scale 1:10, below: draft of object, hand, and cube, design of a monument, 1975
Karton, Bleistift, roter, blauer, gelber Buntstift Cardboard, pencil, red, blue, yellow crayon
24 x 31,5 cm
Inv.-Nr. K.I. 15154/43* Seite Page 60

Waffenmuseum Museum of Ancient Weapons Castello di Brescia, Piazza dei Martiri, Brescia
2 Entwurfskartons, zusammengefügt, mit maßgetreuen Details der Stäbe mit Gelenkverbindungen und Bohrlöchern 2 sheets of cardboard, joined, with true-to-scale details of the poles, with joints and drill holes, 1971
Papier, Bleistift, roter, orange Buntstift, grüner Filzstift Paper, pencil, red, orange crayon, green felt tip
21 x 39,7 cm (1,2,3); 22 x 28 cm (4)
Inv.-Nr. K.I. 15154/44* Seite Page 59

Tisch und Sessel für Luigi Nono Table and chair for Luigi Nono
Konstruktionsskizzen für Sessel und Tisch mit Details, Maßangaben, Maßstab 1:2 Construction sketches with details and measurements, scale 1:2
Entwurfskarton, Bleistift, roter Buntstift Cardboard, pencil, red crayon
52 x 70 cm
Inv.-Nr. K.I. 15154/45*

Kleiderschrank und Bibliothek für Nini Scarpa Wardrobe and library for Nini Scarpa
Querschnitt und Aufriss des Kleiderschranks und Bücherregals mit Schiebetürunatersatz, mit Maßangaben, o. J. Cross-section and elevation of wardrobe and bookshelf with sliding door support, with measurements, undated
Entwurfskarton, Bleistift Cardboard, pencil
23 x 35 cm
Inv.-Nr. K.I. 15154/46

Architekturfakultät der Universität Venedig Department of Architecture, Venice University, Aula Magna di Ca' Fascari
Ausstellungsinstallation, Aufriss, Wandablauf und Grundriss des Ausstellungsraumes mit Anlage der Hängung der Gemälde, handschriftliche Vermerke, 1960 Exhibition installation, elevation, wall sequence and ground plan of exhibition space with details concerning the hanging of the paintings, handwritten notes, 1960
Planpause, Bleistift, blauer, roter, orange, rosa Buntstift Blueprint, pencil, blue, red, orange, pink crayon
31,5 x 68,5 cm
Inv.-Nr. K.I. 15154/47/1*
Seite Page 64

Architekturfakultät der Universität Venedig Department of Architecture, Venice University, Aula Magna di Ca' Foscari
Ausstellungsinstallation, Entwurf für den Wandablauf mit angedeuteter Hängung der Gemälde und mit Besuchern Exhibition installation, design for wall sequence with outlines of the hanging of the paintings and with visitors, 1954–56
Entwurfspapier, Bleistift, orange, gelber, blauer Buntstift Sketching paper, pencil, orange, yellow, blue crayon
29,7 x 77 cm
Inv.-Nr. K.I. 15154/47/2*
Seite Page 65

Architekturfakultät der Universität Venedig Department of Architecture, Venice University, Aula Magna di Ca' Foscari
Ausstellungsinstallation, Detailzeichnungen der Verbindungen in Holz und Stahl und der Stützen, Planpausen, Korrekturen mit Bleistift, 4 Blatt, ein Blatt doppelseitig, o. J. Exhibition installation, detail drawings of wood and steel connections and supports, blueprints, pencil revisions, 4 sheets, one sheet recto and verso, undated
Je Each 33 x 22 cm
Inv.-Nr. K.I. 15154/47/3–6

Tomba Brion, San Vito d'Altivole
Doppelseitig bezeichnetes Blatt mit Bleistiftskizzen zu Durchmesser und Verbindungen der Rundstäbe Drawings of diameter and connections of round bars on recto and verso, 1970–78
Entwurfspapier, Bleistift Sketching paper, pencil
Je Each 28 x 22 cm
Inv.-Nr. K.I. 15154/48, 15154/49

Ausstellungsschrank für die Triennale di Milano Exhibition showcase for the Triennale di Milano
Aufriss, Grundriss, Maßstab 1:10 Elevation, top view, scale 1:10
Bleistiftskizze auf der Rückseite, Planpause, Korrekturen mit Bleistift Verso with pencil sketch, blueprint, pencil revisions
55,2 x 47,7 cm
Inv.-Nr. K.I. 15154/50

Haus Golin Golin House, Montecchio Maggiore
Eingangsbereich mit halbrund angelegter Tür und dem Korridor, Maßstab 1:10 Entrance area with semicircular door and corridor, scale 1:10, 1977/78
Planpause mit Bleistiftkorrekturen Blueprint with pencil revisions
46 x 65,5 cm
Inv.-Nr. K.I. 15154/51/1*

Haus Golin Golin House, Montecchio Maggiore
Eingangsbereich mit halbrund angelegter Tür und dem Korridor Entrance area with semicircular door and corridor, 1977/78
Planpause Blueprint
46 x 65,5 cm
Inv.-Nr. K.I. 15154/51/2*

Haus Golin Golin House, Montecchio Maggiore
Planpause mit Bleistiftskizzen Blueprint with pencil sketches, 1977/78
54,5 x 73,5 cm
Inv.-Nr. K.I. 15154/51/3

Haus Golin Golin House, Montecchio Maggiore
Details der Türkonstruktion des Eingangs Details of entrance door construction, 1977/78
Planpausen, teilweise collagiert, mit Buntstiftkorrekturen Blueprints, partly collaged, with crayon revisions
29,5 x 21 cm (4, 5); 49,5 x 34 cm (6)
Inv.-Nr. K.I. 15154/51/4–6

Haus Golin Golin House, Montecchio Maggiore
Planpause auf Entwurfspapier, mit Bleistiftkorrekturen Blueprint on sketching paper, with pencil revisions, 1977/78
25,2 x 63 cm
Inv.-Nr. K.I. 15154/51/7

4 Entwurfszeichnungen 4 design drawings
Entwürfe für Konstruktionsdetails, o. J. Sketches of construction details, undated
Schreibpapier, Bleistift, gelber, grüner, roter Buntstift Writing paper, pencil, yellow, green, red crayon
Je Each 29,5 x 21 cm
Inv.-Nr. K.I. 15154/52*

3 Entwurfsblätter 3 design sheets
2 farbig ausgearbeitete Plankopien mit Entwürfen für Schraubverbindungen, 1 Blatt mit der Vorlage für Betonschalung [Tomba Brion?], dieses Blatt auch mit Bleistiftskizze auf der Rückseite, o. J. 2 colored blueprints with designs of screw connections, 1 sheet with model for concrete planking [Tomba Brion?], this sheet with pencil sketch on verso, undated
Schreibpapier, Kopien, teilweise mit gelbem, rotem, orange, blauem Farbstift überarbeitet Writing paper, partly revised (yellow, red, orange, blue crayon)
Je Each 33 x 21,5 cm
Inv.-Nr. K.I. 15154/53, 15154/54*, 15154/55

Kommode für Nini Scarpa Chest of drawers for Nini Scarpa
Karton mit Vorzeichnung der Konstruktion der Kommode (Ladenauszüge) sowie der Front, Karton, Planpause mit in rotem, grünem, gelbem Buntstift angelegten Korrekturen und handschriftlichen Vermerken in Bleistift und Kugelschreiber für Material und Maße, o. J. Draft of construction with drawer and front details, cardboard, blueprint with red, green, yellow crayon revisions and handwritten pencil and ballpoint material specifications and measurements, undated
50 x 70 cm
Inv.-Nr. K.I. 15154/56

Entwurf für Kommode unter einem Fenster Design for a chest of drawers below a window
Skizze zur Kommode und zu Material und Anschluss zum Fenster, mit Maßangaben, o. J. Sketch with details on material and connection with window, measurements
Entwurfspapier, Bleistift Sketching paper, pencil, undated
29,5 x 52 cm
Inv.-Nr. K.I. 15154/57

Tomba Brion, San Vito d'Altivole
Ansicht des Wandablaufs des Pavillons mit als „Modulor" genutzter Skizze einer weiblichen Figur, mit Maßangaben View of pavilion wall sequence with sketch of a female figure used as "modulor," with measurements, 1970–78
Karton mit Planpause, mit blauem, orange, gelbem, grünem Buntstift gehöht, ergänzende Bleistiftskizzen Cardboard with blueprint, heightened with blue, orange, yellow, green crayon, additional pencil sketches
43 x 70,5 cm
Inv.-Nr. K.I. 15154/58
Seite Page 81

Tomba Brion, San Vito d'Altivole
Detailzeichnungen für die Verschlüsse der Kassette zum Kruzifix der Tomba Brion Detail drawings for lock of crucifix box, 1970–78
Aquafix, Japan, Bleistift Aquafix, japan, pencil
59,5 x 92 cm (1), 21 x 29,7 cm (2)
Inv.-Nr. K.I. 15154/59/1, 2

Tomba Brion, San Vito d'Altivole
Bleistiftzeichnung auf Velin Pencil drawing on vellum paper, 1970–78
17,5 x 22 cm
Inv.-Nr. K.I. 15154/60

Museo Correr, Venedig Venice
Skizze mit farbig angelegten Flächen Sketch with colored areas, 1953
Papier, Bleistift, roter, orange, gelber, Buntstift Paper, pencil, red, orange, yellow crayon
28 x 22 cm
Inv.-Nr. K.I. 15154/61

Tomba Brion, San Vito d'Altivole
Details der Innengestaltung der Kassette für das Kruzifix der Kappelle Details of interior design of the crucifix box for the chapel, 1970–78
Velin, Bleistift Vellum paper, pencil
30 x 27 cm
Inv.-Nr. K.I. 15154/62* Seite Page 88 oben top

Palazzo Querini Stampalia, Venedig Venice
Doppelseitiges Blatt mit Skizzen für den Querschnitt und die Form des Handlaufs der Zugangsbrücke Sheet with sketches of cross-section and form of access bridge handrail, recto and verso, 1961–63
Papier, Bleistift, Filzstift Paper, pencil, felt tip
31,5 x 21,5 cm
Inv.-Nr. K.I. 15154/63* Seite Page 46

Palazzo Querini Stampalia, Venedig Venice
Skizze für die Besucherbänke, mit Material- und Maßangaben Sketch of the visitor benches, with material specifications and measurements, 1961–63
Entwurfspapier, Bleistift, orange, gelber Buntstift Sketching paper, pencil, orange, yellow crayon
21 x 30 cm
Inv.-Nr. K.I. 15154/64* Seite Page 53

Palazzo Querini Stampalia, Venedig Venice
Planpause mit Bleistiftkorrekturen und Maßangaben, Maßstab 1:10, Skizzen verso Blueprint with pencil revisions and measurements, scale 1:10, with sketches on verso, 1961–63
Bleistift, rosa Farbstift, Kugelschreiber Pencil, pink crayon, ballpoint
41 x 100,5 cm
Inv.-Nr. K.I. 15154/65

Tomba Brion, San Vito d'Altivole
Querschnitt mit Materialangaben und Aufbauzeichnung, Oktober 1973 Cross-section with material specification and structural drawing, October 1973
Planpause, Bleistift, roter, gelber, blauer Buntstift Blueprint, pencil, red, yellow, blue crayon
93 x 33,6 cm
Inv.-Nr. K.I. 15154/66

Tomba Brion, San Vito d'Altivole
Handzeichnung Carlo Scarpas für die Flächenaufteilung der Wände, mit Maßangaben Sketch by Carlo Scarpa for distribution of wall areas, with measurements, 1970–78
Papier, Bleistift, grüner, gelber Filzstift Paper, pencil, green, yellow felt tip
21 x 29,7 cm
Inv.-Nr. K.I. 15154/67* Seite Page 78 unten bottom

Tomba Brion, San Vito d'Altivole
Aufriss und Grundriss mit Maß- und Materialangaben Elevation and ground plan with measurements and material specifications, 1970–78
Planpause, Bleistift, roter, blauer Kugelschreiber Blueprint, pencil, red, blue ballpoint
Je Each 41,2 x 100 cm
Inv.-Nr. K.I. 15154/68/1, 2* Seite Page 83, 84

Palazzo Querini Stampalia, Venedig Venice
5 Skizzen für den Querschnitt und die Form des Handlaufs der Zugangsbrücke 5 sketches of cross-section and form of access bridge handrail, 1961–63
Velin, Bleistift, gelber, brauner Buntstift Vellum paper, pencil, yellow, brown crayon
Je Each 23,5 x 23,5 cm
Inv.-Nr. K.I. 15154/71–74/1, 2* Seite Page 44/45

Palazzo Querini Stampalia, Venedig Venice
Querschnitt der Fensterbank und Aufriss eines Fensters, mit Maßangaben Cross-section of window seat and elevation of a window, with measurements, 1961–63
Planpause, Bleistift, roter Buntstift Blueprint, pencil, red crayon
37,7 x 42 cm
Inv.-Nr. K.I. 15154/75* Seite Page 49

Palazzo Querini Stampalia, Venedig Venice
Entwurf für die Brücke über den Kanal zum Eingang, mit Bleistift- und Buntstiftkorrekturen und Maßangaben Sketch for the access bridge over the canal, with pencil and crayon revisions and measurements, 1961–63
Planpause, Bleistift, roter Buntstift Blueprint, pencil, red crayon
58 x 100 cm
Inv.-Nr. K.I. 15154/76/1* Seite Page 41

Palazzo Querini Stampalia, Venedig Venice
Entwurf für die Brücke über den Kanal zum Eingang, mit Maßangaben Sketch for the access bridge over the canal, with measurements, 1961–63
Planpause mit Bleistiftkorrekturen Blueprint with pencil revisions
58 x 100 cm
Inv.-Nr. K.I. 15154/76/2* Seite Page 43

Palazzo Querini Stampalia, Venedig Venice
Bleistiftzeichnung mit Maßangaben, Maßstab 1:5 Pencil drawing with measurements, scale 1:5, 1961–63
2 collagierte Zeichenpapierblätter, Bleistift, roter, blauer Buntstift 2 collaged sheets of drawing paper, red, blue crayon
31,5 x 86,5 cm
Inv.-Nr. K.I. 15154/77*

Olivetti-Schauraum, Venedig Olivetti showroom, Venice
Perspektive und Aufriss der Gitterwände mit Materialangaben und Konstruktionsdetails des Schiebemechanismus, Bleistiftzeichnung verso Perspective and elevation of walls with material specifications and construction details of sliding mechanism, verso with pencil drawing, 1957/58
Planpause, Bleistift Blueprint, pencil
Je Each 44,5 x 61,5 cm
Inv.-Nr. K.I. 15154/78, 15154/79

Tomba Brion, San Vito d'Altivole
Ansicht des Wandablaufs des Pavillons mit Skizzen des Kopfes Carlo Scarpas, seiner Frau Nini und seines Sohnes Tobia, mit Maßangaben View of pavilion wall sequence with sketches of the head of Carlo Scarpa, his wife Nini and his son Tobia, with measurements, 1970–78
Planpause, mit rotem Buntstift gehöht, ergänzende Bleistiftskizzen Blueprint, heightened with red crayon, additional pencil sketches
Je Each 43 x 70,5 cm
Inv.-Nr. K.I. 15154/80*, 15154/81 Seite Page 80 oben top

Tomba Brion, San Vito d'Altivole
Aufriss mit Maßangaben, November 1973 Elevation with measurements, November 1973
Planpause, Bleistift Blueprint, pencil
54,7 x 26 cm
Inv.-Nr. K.I. 15154/82

Tomba Brion, San Vito d'Altivole
Aufriss mit Maßangaben, Maßstab 1:10 Elevation with measurements, scale 1:10, 1970–78
Planpause, Bleistift, orange, gelber Buntstift, grüner Filzstift Blueprint, pencil, orange, yellow crayon, green felt tip
67 x 108, 5 cm
Inv.-Nr. K.I. 15154/83*

Tomba Brion, San Vito d'Altivole
Querschnitt mit Materialangaben und Maßen, Maßstab 1:5, Juli 1974 Cross-section with material specifications and measurements, scale 1:5, July 1974
Planpause, Bleistift Blueprint, pencil
48,5 x 73,5 cm
Inv.-Nr. K.I. 15154/84*

Tomba Brion, San Vito d'Altivole
Aufriss mit Maß- und Materialangaben Elevation with measurements and material specifications, 1970–78
Zeichenkarton, Bleistift, orange, gelber Buntstift, grüner Filzstift Cardboard, pencil, orange, yellow crayon, green felt tip
70 x 100,5 cm
Inv.-Nr. K.I. 15154/85*

Tomba Brion, San Vito d'Altivole
Grundriss, farbig korrigiert, Aufsicht, Maßangaben Ground plan with measurements and revisions in color, 1970–78
Planpause, Bleistift, mit rotem, gelbem, rosa, grünem Buntstift gehöht Blueprint, pencil, heightened with red, yellow, pink, green crayon
43 x 70,5 cm
Inv.-Nr. K.I. 15154/86*

Tomba Brion, San Vito d'Altivole
Luster der Kapelle, Originalzeichnung, mit Maß- und Materialangaben, zwei Kopfstudien Chandelier of the chapel, study of two heads, original drawing with measurements and material specifications, 1970–78
Zeichenkarton, Bleistift, mit orange, gelbem Buntstift gehöht Cardboard, pencil, heightened with orange, yellow crayon
100 x 35 cm
Inv.-Nr. K.I. 15154/87* Seite Page 79

Tomba Brion, San Vito d'Altivole
Grundriss mit Maß- und Materialangaben, Maßstab 1:10 Ground plan with measurements and material specifications, scale 1:10, 1970–78
Planpause, orange, gelber, brauner Buntstift Blueprint, pencil, orange, red, yellow, brown crayon
55 x 90 cm
Inv.-Nr. K.I. 15154/88* Seite Page 85

Olivetti-Schauraum, Venedig Olivetti showroom, Venice
Perspektive und Aufriss einer Kommode mit Materialangaben und Maßen sowie Konstruktionsdetails, Maßstab 1:10 Perspective and elevation of a chest of drawers with material specifications, measurements, and details of construction, scale 1:10, 1957/58
Zeichenkarton, Bleistift, roter Buntstift Cardboard, pencil, red crayon
44,5 x 61,5 cm
Inv.-Nr. K.I. 15154/89

Palazzo Querini Stampalia, Venedig Venice
Bleistiftzeichnung mit Maßangaben Drawing with measurements, 1961–63
Zeichenkarton, Bleistift Cardboard, pencil
39,2 x 100 cm
Inv.-Nr. K.I. 15154/90

Gipsoteca Canoviana, Possagno
Querschnitte und Aufsicht der Böden mit Konstruktionsdetails und Form der Schrauben, mit Maßangaben, Skizze in Buntstift auf der Rückseite Cross-sections and top view of floor with details of construction and form of screws, with measurements, verso with crayon sketch, 1955–57
Beiges Packpapier, Bleistift, roter Buntstift (verso) Beige wrapping paper, pencil, red crayon on verso
Je Each 54 x 70,5 cm
Inv.-Nr. K.I. 15154/91*, 15154/92 Seite Page 55, 57

Tomba Brion, San Vito d'Altivole
Ansicht des Wandablaufs des Pavillons mit Skizze einer weiblichen Figur, mit Maßangaben View of pavilion wall sequence with sketch of female figure, with measurements, 1970–78
Planpause, farbig korrigiert, mit rotem, blauem, orange Buntstift gehöht, ergänzende Bleistiftskizzen Blueprint with revisions in color, heightened with red, blue, orange crayon, additional pencil sketches
51,2 x 102,5 cm
Inv.-Nr. K.I. 15154/93*, 15154/94–97 Seite Page 82

Gipsoteca Canoviana, Possagno
Querschnitte und Aufsicht der Profile der Türen und Fenster, mit Maß- und Materialangaben Cross-sections and top view of door and window profiles, with measurements and material specifications, 1955–57
Plankopie, Bleistift, roter Buntstift (verso) Blueprint, pencil, red crayon on verso
58 x 168 cm
Inv.-Nr. K.I. 15154/98* Seite Page 56

Tomba Brion, San Vito d'Altivole
Originalzeichnung für den Rahmen der Betonschiebetüren, farbig gehöht mit Skizze einer weiblichen Figur, Maßangaben und Konstruktionsdetails Original drawing of frame for concrete sliding doors with sketch of female figure, measurements, and construction details, 1970–78
Bleistiftzeichnung auf dünnem Karton, mit rotem, grünem, gelbem Buntstift und grünem, gelbem, rosa, orange, blauem, braunem Filzstift gehöht, ergänzende Bleistiftskizzen Pencil on thin cardboard, heightened with red, green, yellow crayon and green, yellow, pink, orange, blue, brown felt tip, additional pencil sketches
99 x 211 cm
Inv.-Nr. K.I. 15154/99 Seite Page 74

Tomba Brion, San Vito d'Altivole
Entwurf für das Siegel der Brion, mit Querschnitten Design for the Brion family's seal, with cross-sections, 1970–78
Velin, Bleistift Vellum paper, pencil
29,5 x 60 cm
Inv.-Nr. K.I. 15154/100/1

Tomba Brion, San Vito d'Altivole
Entwurf für das Siegel der Brion, mit Querschnitten Design for the Brion family's seal, with cross-sections, 1970–78
Planpause auf Papier Blueprint on paper
51 x 39 cm
Inv.-Nr. K.I. 15154/100/2

Tomba Brion, San Vito d'Altivole
Rahmen und Profile der Fenster, mit Bleistift korrigiert, mit Maß- und Materialangaben Frame and window profiles, pencil revisions, with measurements and material specifications, 1970–78
Planpause, Bleistift Blueprint, pencil
34 x 74,5 cm
Inv.-Nr. K.I. 15154/101

Tomba Brion, San Vito d'Altivole
Entwurf für die Doppelwand des Pavillons, mit Querschnitt und Aufsicht Design for double pavilion wall, with cross-section and top view, 1970–78
Planpause auf Velin, Bleistiftkorrekturen Blueprint on vellum paper, pencil revisions
42 x 59,7 cm
Inv.-Nr. K.I. 15154/102

Tomba Brion, San Vito d'Altivole
Zeichnung mit verschiedenen Buchstabenentwürfen für die Beschriftung der Sarkophage der Familie Brion Drawing with various letter designs for the inscription of the Brion family's sarcophagi, 1970–78
Entwurfspapier, Bleistift, grüner Filzstift Sketching paper, pencil, green felt tip
21 x 29,7 cm
Inv.-Nr. K.I. 15154/103

Tomba Brion, San Vito d'Altivole
Originalzeichnung für den Rahmen der Tomba Brion Original drawing of framework, 1970–78
Entwurfspapier, Bleistift Sketching paper, pencil
22 x 28 cm
Inv.-Nr. K.I. 15154/104

Tomba Brion, San Vito d'Altivole
Originalzeichnung für die Paneele der Fassade des Pavillons, mit Querschnitt, mit Maß- und Materialangaben Original drawing of panels for the pavilion facade, with cross-section, measurements, and material specifications, 1970–78
Entwurfspapier, Bleistift, mit rotem, gelbem Buntstift gehöht Sketching paper, pencil drawing, heightened with crayon
29,5 x 21 cm
Inv.-Nr. K.I. 15154/105

Tomba Brion, San Vito d'Altivole
Originalzeichnung für die Scharniere der Schiebetüren der Tomba Brion, mit Querschnitten Original drawing of sliding door hinges, with cross-sections, 1970–78
Entwurfspapier, Bleistift mit rotem, gelbem Buntstift gehöht Sketching paper, pencil drawing, heightened with yellow and red crayon
29,5 x 21 cm
Inv.-Nr. K.I. 15154/106*

Tomba Brion, San Vito d'Altivole
Eckpaneele der Fassade des Pavillons, mit Querschnitt, Maß- und Materialangaben Corner panels of pavilion facade, with cross-section, measurements, and material specifications, 1970–78
Plankopie, mit Bleistift korrigiert Blueprint with pencil revisions
42 x 69,5 cm
Inv.-Nr. K.I. 15154/107

Tomba Brion, San Vito d'Altivole
Plankopie mit Bleistiftkorrekturen, mit Maß- und Materialangaben Blueprint with pencil revisions, with measurements and material specifications, 1970–78
79,5 x 43 cm
Inv.-Nr. K.I. 15154/108

Tomba Brion, San Vito d'Altivole
Ansicht des Wandablaufs des Pavillons, mit Maßangaben View of pavilion wall sequence with measurements, 1970–78
Planpause, ergänzende Bleistiftskizzen Blueprint, additional pencil sketches
42 x 59, 5 cm
Inv.-Nr. K.I. 15154/109

Tomba Brion, San Vito d'Altivole
Ansicht des Wandablaufs des Pavillons, mit Maßangaben View of pavilion wall sequence, with measurements, 1970–78
Planpause, ergänzende Bleistiftskizzen Blueprint, additional pencil sketches
42,5 x 59,5 cm
Inv.-Nr. K.I. 15154/110*

Tomba Brion, San Vito d'Altivole
Tür der Kapelle, kolorierte Originalzeichnung, mit Konstruktions- und Maßdetailangaben Chapel door, colored original drawing, with detailed construction specifications and measurements, 1970–78
Zeichenkarton, Bleistift, roter, gelber, orange, blauer Buntstift Cardboard, pencil, red, yellow, orange, blue crayon
63,5 x 99,5 cm
Inv.-Nr. K.I. 15154/111*   Seite Page 75

Tomba Brion, San Vito d'Altivole
Aufriss mit Maß- und Materialangaben, Maßstab 1:2, handschriftliche Vermerke Carlo Scarpas Elevation with measurements and material specifications, scale 1:2, handwritten notes by Carlo Scarpa, 1970–78
Planpause, Bleistift, gelber Buntstift Blueprint, pencil, yellow crayon
48,5 x 73,2 cm
Inv.-Nr. K.I. 15154/112

Tomba Brion, San Vito d'Altivole
Querschnitte der Sarkophage, freie Skizzen Carlo Scarpas, doppelseitig Cross-sections of sarcophagi, recto and verso with freehand sketches by Carlo Scarpa, 1970–78
Papier, Bleistift Paper, pencil
20,7 x 29,7 cm
Inv.-Nr. K.I. 15154/113

Tomba Brion, San Vito d'Altivole
Messingzwingen für die Konstruktion der Sarkophage, freie Skizzen Carlo Scarpas für die Konstruktion Brass clamps for sarcophagi, freehand sketches for the construction by Carlo Scarpa, 1970–78
Velin, 2 Blatt mit Klebeband collagiert, Bleistift, gelber, orange, rosa Buntstift Vellum paper, 2 sheets collaged with adhesive tape, pencil, yellow, orange, pink crayon
32 x 27 cm
Inv.-Nr. K.I. 15154/114

Tomba Brion, San Vito d'Altivole
Messingrahmen für die Sarkophage, freie Skizzen Carlo Scarpas für die Konstruktion, mit Maßangaben, doppelseitig Brass frames for sarcophagi, freehand sketches for the construction by Carlo Scarpa, with measurements, recto and verso, 1970–78
Papier, Bleistift Paper, pencil
22 x 28,5 cm
Inv.-Nr. K.I. 15154/115

Tomba Brion, San Vito d'Altivole
Stirnseite der Sarkophage, freie Skizzen Carlo Scarpas für die Konstruktion, mit Maßangaben Front of sarcophagi, freehand sketches for the construction by Carlo Scarpa, with measurements, 1970–78
Planpause, Bleistift, gelber, orange Buntstift Blueprint, pencil, yellow, orange crayon
33 x 21,5 cm
Inv.-Nr. K.I. 15154/116, 15154/117

Tomba Brion, San Vito d'Altivole
Messingbänder für die Sarkophage, freie Skizzen Carlo Scarpas für die Konstruktion, mit Details der Verankerung im Marmor, mit Maßangaben Brass frame for sarcophagi, freehand sketches for the construction by Carlo Scarpa, with measurements, recto and verso, 1970–78
Planpause Blueprint
33 x 21,5 cm
Inv.-Nr. K.I. 15154/118

Tomba Brion, San Vito d'Altivole
Stirnseite der Sarkophage, mit Maßangaben Front of sarcophagi, with measurements, 1970–78
Planpause Blueprint
33 x 21,5 cm
Inv.-Nr. K.I. 15154/119

Tomba Brion, San Vito d'Altivole
Längsseite der Sarkophage, mit Maßangaben Long side of sarcophagi, with measurements, 1970–78
Planpause Blueprint
21,5 x 33 cm
Inv.-Nr. K.I. 15154/120

Tomba Brion, San Vito d'Altivole
Messingrahmen für die Sarkophage, freie Skizzen Carlo Scarpas für die Konstruktion, mit Maßangaben, eigenhändige Zeichnung Carlo Scarpas, signiert Brass frame for sarcophagi, freehand sketches for the construction by Carlo Scarpa, with measurements, signed, 1970–78
Papier, Bleistift, gelber, blauer Buntstift Paper, pencil, yellow, blue crayon
21,5 x 33 cm
Inv.-Nr. K.I. 15154/121, 15154/122

Tomba Brion, San Vito d'Altivole
Stirnseite der Sarkophage, mit Maßangaben und Korrekturen Front of sarcophagi, with measurements and revisions, 1970–78
Planpause, gelber Buntstift Blueprint, yellow crayon
21,5 x 33 cm
Inv.-Nr. K.I. 15154/123

Tomba Brion, San Vito d'Altivole
Querschnitte der Sarkophage, freie Skizzen Carlo Scarpas, doppelseitig
Cross-sections of sarcophagi, recto and verso with freehand sketches by
Carlo Scarpa, 1970–78
Karton, Bleistift, gelber Buntstift Cardboard, pencil, yellow crayon
Je Each 21 x 15 cm
Inv.-Nr. K.I. 15154/124, 15154/125

Tomba Brion, San Vito d'Altivole
Stirn- und Längsseite der Sarkophage, korrigiert Front and long side of sarcophagi, with revisions, 1970–78
Planpause, Bleistift Blueprint, pencil
27 x 93,5 cm
Inv.-Nr. K.I. 15154/126

Tomba Brion, San Vito d'Altivole
Querschnitte des Fußbretts des Altars der Kapelle, doppelseitig, März 1974
Cross-section of footboard for the altar of the chapel, recto and verso, March 1974
Planpause nach Skizze Carlo Scarpas Blueprint after sketch by Carlo Scarpa
37,7 x 59 cm
Inv.-Nr. K.I. 15154/127

Tomba Brion, San Vito d'Altivole
Struktive Details Structural details, 1970–78
Planpause auf Velin Blueprint on vellum paper
40,5 x 100,5 cm
Inv.-Nr. K.I. 15154/128

Tomba Brion, San Vito d'Altivole
Struktive Details, mit Maßangaben Structural details, with measurements, 1970–78
Planpause auf Papier, Bleistift, roter, grüner, orange Buntstift Blueprint on paper, pencil, red, green, orange crayon
25,7 x 132,5 cm
Inv.-Nr. K.I. 15154/129

Tomba Brion, San Vito d'Altivole
Struktive Details, mit Bleistift von Carlo Scarpa korrigiert Structural details, with pencil corrections by Carlo Scarpa, 1970–78
Planpause auf Papier, Bleistift Blueprint on paper, pencil
29,5 x 60 cm
Inv.-Nr. K.I. 15154/130

Tomba Brion, San Vito d'Altivole
Struktive Details, mit Bleistift von Carlo Scarpa korrigiert Structural details, with pencil corrections by Carlo Scarpa, 1970–78
Planpause auf Papier, Bleistift, roter, gelber Buntstift Blueprint on paper, pencil, red, yellow crayon
30 x 55 cm
Inv.-Nr. K.I. 15154/131/1

Tomba Brion, San Vito d'Altivole
Struktive Details, mit Bleistift und Filzstift von Carlo Scarpa korrigiert, Bleistiftskizze auf der Rückseite Structural details, with pencil and felt tip revisions by Carlo Scarpa, pencil sketch on verso, 1970–78
Planpause auf Papier, Bleistift, roter, blauer, gelber Buntstift, Filzstift
Blueprint on paper, pencil, red, blue, yellow crayon, felt tip
30 x 55 cm
Inv.-Nr. K.I. 15154/131/2

Tomba Brion, San Vito d'Altivole
Querschnitte der Türscharniere Cross-sections of door hinges, 1970–78
Planpause auf Papier, von Carlo Scarpa mit rotem, gelbem, blauem Buntstift koloriert Blueprint on paper, colored with red, yellow, blue crayon by Carlo Scarpa
34,5 x 61 cm
Inv.-Nr. K.I. 15154/132*
Seite Page 77

Tomba Brion, San Vito d'Altivole
Plankopie mit Originalzeichnung Carlo Scarpas auf der Rückseite, Kopie mit Buntstift von Scarpa gehöht, mit struktiven Details für die Verbindungen der Wandstützen des Pavillons Blueprint with original drawing by Carlo Scarpa on verso, blueprint heightened with crayon by the architect, with structural details for the connections between pavilion walls and supports, 1970–78
3 zusammengeklebte Papiere, Bleistift, roter, gelber, blauer Buntstift 3 sheets of paper glued together, pencil, red, yellow, blue crayon
34,7 x 61 cm
Inv.-Nr. K.I. 15154/133*

Tomba Brion, San Vito d'Altivole
Querschnitte des Fußbretts des Altars der Kapelle, Februar 1974
Cross-sections of footboard for the altar of the chapel, February 1974
Plankopie nach Skizze Carlo Scarpas Blueprint after sketch by Carlo Scarpa
37,5 x 130,5 cm
Inv.-Nr. K.I. 15154/134

Tomba Brion, San Vito d'Altivole
Querschnitte der Tür der Kapelle, mit Bleistiftkorrekturen, Februar 1974
Cross-sections of chapel door, with pencil revisions, February 1974
Plankopie nach Skizze Carlo Scarpas Blueprint after sketch by Carlo Scarpa
50 x 101 cm
Inv.-Nr. K.I. 15154/135

Tomba Brion, San Vito d'Altivole
Querschnitte der Scharniere der Tür der Kapelle, Maßstab 1:1, Februar 1974
Cross-sections of hinges for the chapel door, scale 1:1, February 1974
Plankopie nach Skizze Carlo Scarpas, Bleistift Blueprint after sketch by Carlo Scarpa, pencil
74 x 37,5 cm
Inv.-Nr. K.I. 15154/136

Tomba Brion, San Vito d'Altivole
Querschnitte des Altars der Kapelle Cross-sections of the altar for the chapel, 1970–78
Plankopie nach Skizze Carlo Scarpas, von ihm mit rotem, gelbem Buntstift gehöht und korrigiert Blueprint after sketch by Carlo Scarpa, heightened and revised by the architect with red, yellow crayon
30 x 76 cm
Inv.-Nr. K.I. 15154/137

Tomba Brion, San Vito d'Altivole
Beschriftung der Sarkophage, Schriftprobe zur Umsetzung in Elfenbein, Originalzeichnung mit Maßangaben Inscription for sarcophagi, specimen for execution in ivory, original drawing with measurements, 1970–78
Velin, Bleistift Vellum paper, pencil
31,5 x 47,5 cm
Inv.-Nr. K.I. 15154/138/1*
Seite Page 87 oben top

Tomba Brion, San Vito d'Altivole
Beschriftung der Sarkophage, Schriftprobe zur Umsetzung in Elfenbein im Ebenholzrahmen, Plankopie und Originalzeichnung mit Maßangaben, Maßstab 1:10, 1:5 Inscription for sarcophagi, specimen for execution in ivory in ebony frame, original drawing with measurements, scales 1:10, 1:5, 1970–78
Plankopie, Bleistift Blueprint, pencil
26,5 x 77 cm
Inv.-Nr. K.I. 15154/138/2*

Tomba Brion, San Vito d'Altivole
Aufsicht der Deckenkonstruktion, mit Maßangaben, Maßstab 1:25
Top view of ceiling construction, with measurements, scale 1:25, 1970–78
Plankopie nach Originalzeichnung Carlo Scarpas, mit Bunt- und Bleistiftkorrekturen Blueprint on paper after original drawing by Carlo Scarpa, with pencil and crayon revisions
26 x 132,5 cm
Inv.-Nr. K.I. 15154/139

Haus Carlo Scarpa, Venedig, Rio Marin
House Carlo Scarpa, Venice, Rio Marin
Detailzeichnung für die Konstruktion von Kästchen der Einrichtung des Hauses Carlo Scarpas, mit Widmung an Saverio Anfodillo, Originalmaß Detail drawing for construction of cabinets for furnishing of house, with dedication to Saverio Anfodillo, original dimensions, 1963
Velin, Bleistift Vellum paper, Pencil
34 x 58 cm
Inv.-Nr. K.I. 15154/140*

Tomba Brion, San Vito d'Altivole
Querschnitt des Rahmens und Aufbau der Tür der Kapelle aus Ebenholz mit Rosenholzeinlagen, mit Anlage der Messingtürgriffe, doppelseitig, März 1974 Cross-section of frame and structure of ebony chapel door with rosewood inlays, with brass door handles, recto and verso, March 1974
Plankopie nach Skizze Carlo Scarpas, Bleistift, roter, gelber Buntstift Blueprint after a sketch by Carlo Scarpa, pencil, red, yellow crayon
37,7 x 78 cm
Inv.-Nr. K.I. 15154/141   Seite Page 76

Palazzo Querini Stampalia, Venedig, Tomba Brion et alia
35 Entwurfszeichnungen mit Skizzen für Details, o. J. 35 design drawings with sketches of details, undated
Inv.-Nr. K.I. 15154/142*   Seite Page 48, 63 unten bottom

Tomba Brion, San Vito d'Altivole
Beschriftung der Sarkophage, Schriftprobe zur Umsetzung in Elfenbein im Ebenholzrahmen, Plankopie und Originalzeichnung mit Bleistift, mit Maßangaben, doppelseitig Inscription of sarcophagi, specimen for execution in ivory in ebony frame, blueprint and original pencil drawing with measurements, recto and verso, 1970–78
Plankopie auf 3 Blättern, mit Klebeband collagiert, Bleistift Blueprint on 3 sheets, collaged with adhesive tape
21,5 x 76,5 cm
Inv.-Nr. K.I. 15154/143

Tomba Brion, San Vito d'Altivole
Struktive Details und Maßangaben für den Wandablauf des Pavillons sowie 3 Porträtskizzen von Carlo Scarpa, Nini Scarpa, Tobia Scarpa, mit handschriftlichen Angaben des Architekten Structural details and measurements for the pavilion wall, as well as 3 portrait sketches of Carlo Scarpa, Nini Scarpa, Tobia Scarpa, with handwritten notes by the architect, 1970–78
Planpause auf Papier, Bleistift, roter, blauer, brauner Buntstift Blueprint on paper, pencil, red, blue, brown crayon
29,7 x 41 cm
Inv.-Nr. K.I. 15154/144*   Seite Page 80 unten bottom

Tomba Brion, San Vito d'Altivole
Querschnitt des Rahmens und Aufbau der Tür der Kapelle aus Ebenholz mit Rosenholz- und Metalleinlagen, mit Buntstift gehöht, mit Blei- und Buntstiftkorrekturen, doppelseitig, März 1974 Cross-section of frame and structure of ebony chapel door with rosewood and metal inlays, heightened with crayon, with pencil and crayon revisions, recto and verso, March 1974
Plankopie nach Skizze Carlo Scarpas, Bleistift, roter, gelber Buntstift Blueprint after sketch by Carlo Scarpa, pencil, red, yellow crayon
27,4 x 58 cm
Inv.-Nr. K.I. 15154/145*

Haus Zentner, Zürich Zentner House, Zurich
Konsolen für den Speisesaal mit Material- und Maßangaben, Querschnitte, mit Korrekturen Carlo Scarpas Consoles for dining room, with material specifications and measurements, cross-sections, with revisions by Carlo Scarpa, 1961–66
Planpause, mit Bleistift, orange, grünem Buntstift, Filzstift überzeichnet Pencil, orange, green crayon, felt tip
48 x 100,5 cm
Inv.-Nr. K.I. 15154/146

Haus Zentner, Zürich Zentner House, Zurich
Raumteiler mit Maßangaben, Querschnitte, Originalzeichnung Carlo Scarpas Partition with measurements, cross-sections, original drawing by Carlo Scarpa, 1967/68
Velin, mit Bleistift, orange, grünem, rotem Buntstift gehöht Vellum paper, heightened with pencil and orange, green, red crayon
43 x 59,7 cm
Inv.-Nr. K.I. 15154/147/1

Haus Zentner, Zürich Zentner House, Zurich
Detailskizze für den Raumteiler, Querschnitt, Originalmaß, Zeichnung Carlo Scarpas Sketch of details for partition, cross-section, original dimensions, drawing by Carlo Scarpa, 1967/68
Velin, Bleistift Vellum paper, pencil
29,7 x 50,5 cm
Inv.-Nr. K.I. 15154/147/2   Seite Page 31

Haus Zentner, Zürich Zentner House, Zurich
Detailskizze für den Raumteiler, Querschnitt mit Maßangaben, Originalmaß, Zeichnung Carlo Scarpas Sketch of details for partition, cross-section, original dimensions, drawing by Carlo Scarpa, 1961–66
Velin, Bleistift Vellum paper, pencil
29,5 x 35 cm
Inv.-Nr. K.I. 15154/147/3*

Palazzo Querini Stampalia, Venedig Venice
Detailskizze für die Deckenkonstruktion des Windfangs, Aufsicht, Profile, mit Maß- und Materialangaben, Plankopie mit Zeichnung Carlo Scarpas Sketch of details for ceiling construction of vestibule, top view, profiles, with measurements and material specifications, blueprint with drawing by Carlo Scarpa, 1961–63
Originalzeichnung auf Plankopie, Bleistift, roter, violetter, gelber Buntstift Pencil, red, purple, yellow crayon
Je Each 46,5 x 76 cm
Inv.-Nr. K.I. 15154/48, 15154/149

Palazzo Querini Stampalia, Venedig Venice
Detailskizze für die Tür des Lesesaals, Profile der Konstruktion, mit Maß- und Materialangaben, Plankopie mit Zeichnung Carlo Scarpas, doppelseitig Sketch of details for reading room door, profiles of construction, with measurements and material specifications, blueprint with original drawing by Carlo Scarpa, recto and verso, 1961–63
Bleistift, roter, gelber, blauer Buntstift Pencil, red, yellow, blue crayon
30 x 89 cm
Inv.-Nr. K.I. 15154/150

Palazzo Querini Stampalia, Venedig Venice
6 Detailskizzen für die Profile der Türen, Konstruktion, Querschnitte mit Maßangaben, Originalzeichnungen Carlo Scarpas 6 sketches of details for profiles of doors, construction, cross-sections with measurements, original drawings by Carlo Scarpa, 1961–63
Velin, Bleistift Vellum paper, pencil
15 x 22,2 cm (1), 29,7 x 29,7 cm (2), 29,2 x 69 cm (3), 19 x 35 cm (4), 29 x 5 cm (5), 30 x 41,5 cm (6)
Inv.-Nr. K.I. 15154/151/1–6

Palazzo Querini Stampalia, Venedig Venice
Planpause nach Originalzeichnung Carlo Scarpas für die Deckenleuchten, Details der Konstruktion, Querschnitte mit Maßangaben, doppelseitig, 24. April 1963 Blueprint after original drawing by Carlo Scarpa for ceiling lamps, construction details, cross-sections with measurements, recto and verso, April 24, 1963
32,5 x 75 cm
Inv.-Nr. K.I. 15154/152

Palazzo Querini Stampalia, Venedig Venice
Planpause und Detailskizzen für die Gartentür, Konstruktion, Querschnitte mit Maßangaben, im Maßstab 1:5 Blueprint and sketches of details for garden door, construction, cross-sections with measurements, scale 1:5, recto and verso, 1961–63
Bleistift, roter Buntstift Pencil, red crayon
75 x 52,5 cm
Inv.-Nr. K.I. 15154/153

Palazzo Querini Stampalia, Venedig Venice
Gartentür, Konstruktion, Querschnitte mit Maß- und Materialangaben, Originalmaß Garden door, construction, cross-sections with measurements and material specifications, original dimensions, recto and verso, 1961–63
Planpause, Bleistift, roter Buntstift Blueprint, pencil, red crayon
61 x 54 cm
Inv.-Nr. K.I. 15154/154

Palazzo Querini Stampalia, Venedig Venice
Decke hin zum Kanal, Konstruktion, Querschnitte mit Maß- und Materialangaben, Maßstab 1:10, 24. April 1963 Ceiling towards canal, construction, cross-sections with measurements and material specifications, scale 1:10, April 24, 1963
Planpause nach Originalzeichnung Carlo Scarpas Blueprint after original drawing by Carlo Scarpa
37,3 x 109,5 cm
Inv.-Nr. K.I. 15154/155*   Seite Page 47 oben top

Palazzo Querini Stampalia, Venedig Venice
Detailskizzen für die Profile der Fensterbretter, Konstruktion, Querschnitte, Originalmaß, doppelseitig Sketches of details for window sill profiles, construction, cross-sections, original dimension, recto and verso, 1961–63
Bleistift, orange, gelber, roter Buntstift auf Karton Pencil, orange, yellow, red crayon on cardboard
35,4 x 99,5 cm
Inv.-Nr. K.I. 15154/156

Palazzo Querini Stampalia, Venedig Venice
Gartentür, Konstruktion, Details mit Maß- und Materialangaben, Maßstab 1:10 und Originalmaß Garden door, construction, details with measurements and material specifications, scale 1:10 and original dimensions, recto and verso, 1961–63
Planpause, Originalzeichnung mit Bleistift, rotem Buntstift Blueprint, original drawing with pencil, red crayon
60 x 59,5 cm
Inv.-Nr. K.I. 15154/157*   Seite Page 51

Palazzo Querini Stampalia, Venedig Venice
Aufsicht der Brücke als neuem Zugang Top view of bridge as new access, 1961–63
Planpause nach Originalzeichnung Carlo Scarpas, mit Bleistiftkorrektur Blueprint after original drawing by Carlo Scarpa, with pencil revisions
46,5 x 63 cm
Inv.-Nr. K.I. 15154/158*   Seite Page 47 unten bottom

Palazzo Querini Stampalia, Venedig Venice
Gartentür, Konstruktion, Details mit Maß- und Materialangaben, Maßstab 1:10 und Originalmaß, doppelseitig Garden door, construction, details with measurements and material specifications, scale 1:10 and original dimensions, recto and verso, 1961–63
Planpause mit Bleistiftkorrekturen Carlo Scarpas, roter Buntstift Blueprint with pencil revisions by Carlo Scarpa, red pencil
52,5 x 60 cm
Inv.-Nr. K.I. 15154/159

Palazzo Querini Stampalia, Venedig Venice
Gartentür, Konstruktion, Querschnitte mit Maß- und Materialangaben, Originalmaß Garden door, construction, cross-sections with measurements and material specifications, original dimensions, 1961–63
Planpause, Originalzeichnung mit Bleistift, rotem Buntstift Blueprint, original drawing with pencil, red crayon
60,5 x 59 cm
Inv.-Nr. K.I. 15154/160

Palazzo Querini Stampalia, Venedig Venice
Tür der Servicestiege, Konstruktion, Querschnitte mit Maß- und Materialangaben, Maßstab 1:10 und Originalmaß Door for service staircase, construction, cross-sections with measurements and material specifications, scale 1:10 and original dimensions, 1961–63
Planpause, Originalzeichnung mit Bleistift, rotem, gelbem Buntstift Blueprint, original drawing with pencil, red, yellow crayon
45,5 x 75,5 cm
Inv.-Nr. K.I. 15154/161*   Seite Page 52

Palazzo Querini Stampalia, Venedig Venice
Querschnitt der Rahmenprofile und Beschläge der Fenster, mit Maßangaben Cross-section of window frame profiles and fittings, with measurements, 1961–63
Planpause, Bleistift, roter, gelber, blauer, rosa Buntstift Blueprint, pencil, red, yellow, blue, pink crayon
66,5 x 75 cm
Inv.-Nr. K.I. 15154/162

Palazzo Querini Stampalia, Venedig Venice
Gartentür und Fenster, Konstruktion, Querschnitte, Profile, mit Maß- und Materialangaben, Originalmaß Garden door and windows, construction, cross-sections, profiles, with measurements and material specifications, original dimensions, 1961–63
Planpause, Originalzeichnung mit Bleistift, rotem, gelbem Buntstift Blueprint, original drawing with pencil, red, yellow crayon
60 x 125,5 cm
Inv.-Nr. K.I. 15154/163*

Palazzo Querini Stampalia, Venedig Venice
Tür, Konstruktion, Querschnitte mit Beschlägen, mit Maßangaben Door, construction, cross-sections with fittings, with measurements, 1961–63
Planpause, mit Bleistift, rotem, gelbem, orange Buntstift gehöht bzw. korrigiert Blueprint, heightened or revised with pencil and red, yellow, orange crayon
43,7 x 75,5 cm
Inv.-Nr. K.I. 15154/164

Palazzo Querini Stampalia, Venedig Venice
Detailskizze für die Tür des Lesesaals, Profile der Konstruktion, mit Maß- und Materialangaben, Maßstab 1:10 Sketch of details for reading room door, construction profiles, with measurements and material specifications, scale 1:10, 1961–63
Originalzeichnung auf Plankopie, Filzstift, Bleistift, roter, gelber Buntstift Original drawing on blueprint, felt tip, pencil, red, yellow crayon
61,5 x 76 cm
Inv.-Nr. K.I. 15154/165

Palazzo Querini Stampalia, Venedig Venice
Tür der Servicestiege, Konstruktion, Querschnitte mit Maßangaben Service staircase door, construction, cross-sections with measurements, 1961–63
Planpause, Originalzeichnung mit Kugelschreiber, Bleistift, rotem Buntstift Blueprint, original drawing with ballpoint, pencil, red crayon
60,5 x 87 cm
Inv.-Nr. K.I. 15154/166

Palazzo Querini Stampalia, Venedig Venice
Querschnitte der Rahmenprofile und Beschläge der Fenster Cross-section of window frame profiles and fittings, 1961–63
Planpause, roter Buntstift Blueprint, red pencil
57,7 x 75 cm
Inv.-Nr. K.I. 15154/167

Palazzo Querini Stampalia, Venedig Venice
Originalzeichnung für eine Türfüllung mit vergoldetem Holz, Konstruktion, Querschnitt, Aufsicht, mit Beschlägen, mit Maßangaben, doppelseitig Original drawing of a door panel with gilt wood, construction, cross-section, top view, with fittings, with measurements, recto and verso, 1961–63
Zeichnung auf Zeichenkarton, mit Bleistift, rotem, gelbem, orange, blauem Buntstift gehöht, Filzstiftnotizen vorne und Filzstiftskizze auf der Rückseite Cardboard, heightened with pencil and red, yellow, orange, blue crayon, recto: felt tip notes, verso: felt tip sketch
63,5 x 100 cm
Inv.-Nr. K.I. 15154/168*

Ausstellung Exhibition „Giovanni Bellini", Palazzo Ducale, Venedig Venice
Zeichnung für die Beschriftungstafeln, Schriftproben, Materialangaben, Konstruktion Drawing of text panels, type specimens, material specifications, construction, 1949
Velin, Bleistift Vellum paper, pencil
30,2 x 48 cm
Inv.-Nr. K.I. 15154/169*   Seite Page 62

Biennale di Venezia, Pavillon für Venezuela Venezuelan Pavilion
Originalzeichnung und Planpause für Beschläge, Querschnitte und Material-
angaben Original drawing and blueprint of fittings, cross-sections and
material specifications, 1955/56
Bleistift, blauer, gelber Buntstift auf Velin; Planpause, Bleistift, roter Buntstift
Pencil and blue, yellow crayon on vellum paper; pencil and red crayon
Je Each 42,5 x 72 cm
Inv.-Nr. K.I. 15154/170/1, 2

Biennale di Venezia, Pavillon für Venezuela Venezuelan Pavilion
Bodenplatte, Querschnitte und Materialangaben Base plate, cross sections
and material specifications, 1956
Planpause, orange Buntstift Blueprint, orange crayon
75,5 x 50 cm
Inv.-Nr. K.I. 15154/171

Ausstellungen im Museo Correr und Palazzo Ducale, Venedig Exhibitions in
the Museo Correr and the Palazzo Ducale, Venice
52 Originalskizzen Carlo Scarpas für Ausstellungsgestaltungen, u. a. für die
Neugestaltung des Museo Correr und Ausstellungen im Palazzo Ducale
52 original sketches for the exhibition designs by Carlo Scarpa, such as for
the redesign of the Museo Correr and presentations in the Palazzo Ducale,
1949–59
Velin, Schreibpapier, Bleistift, roter, gelber Buntstift, gelber Filzstift,
Kugelschreiber Vellum paper, writing paper, pencil, red, yellow crayon, yellow
felt tip, ballpoint
22 x 28 cm
Inv.-Nr. K.I. 15154/172/1–52*   Seite Page 63 oben top

Aula Tribunale „Manlio Capitolo", Venedig Venice
Zeichnung der Tafel in Originalgröße, mit Profilen, Material- und Maßangaben
Drawing of plate in original dimensions, with profiles, material specifications
and measurements, 1955
Papier, Bleistift, roter, blauer Buntstift, Kugelschreiber Paper, pencil, red, blue
crayon, ballpoint
74,5 x 139 cm
Inv.-Nr. K.I. 15154/173*

Aula Tribunale „Manlio Capitolo", Venedig Venice
Planpause nach signierter Zeichnung Carlo Scarpas mit Aufsicht der Sessel
in Originalgröße, mit Materialangaben Blueprint after signed drawing by Carlo
Scarpa with top view of chairs in their original dimensions, with material
specifications, 1955
Papier, Bleistift Paper, pencil
74,5 x 77,5 cm
Inv.-Nr. K.I. 15154/174

Aula Tribunale „Manlio Capitolo", Venedig Venice
Planpause nach Zeichnung Carlo Scarpas für die Tür im Maßstab 1:10 mit
Anlage der Beschläge, doppelseitig Blueprint after drawing of door with
fittings by Carlo Scarpa, scale 1:10, recto and verso, 1955
Papier, Bleistift Paper, pencil
59,5 x 74 cm
Inv.-Nr. K.I. 15154/175

Aula Tribunale „Manlio Capitolo", Venedig Venice
Planpause nach signierter Zeichnung Carlo Scarpas mit Aufsicht der Sessel
in Originalgröße und Seitenansicht im Maßstab 1:5, mit Materialangaben
doppelseitig Blueprint after signed drawing by Carlo Scarpa with top view of
chairs in their original dimensions and side view of chairs on a scale of 1:5,
with material specifications on recto and verso, 1955
Papier, Bleistift Paper, pencil
74 x 100,6 cm
Inv.-Nr. K.I. 15154/176

Aula Tribunale „Manlio Capitolo", Venedig Venice
Planpause nach signierter Zeichnung Carlo Scarpas für die Scharniere, Tür im
Originalmaß, mit Anlage der Beschläge Blueprint after drawing of door hinges
with fittings by Carlo Scarpa, door in original size, 1955
Papier, Bleistift Paper, pencil
39,5 x 125 cm
Inv.-Nr. K.I. 15154/177

Aula Tribunale „Manlio Capitolo", Venedig Venice
Planpause nach signierter Zeichnung Carlo Scarpas mit Aufsicht der
Klapptische an den Sesseln für die Anwälte, in Originalgröße, mit
Materialangaben doppelseitig Blueprint after signed drawing by Carlo Scarpa
with top view of foldaway tables for the counsels' chairs, original dimensions,
with material specifications on recto and verso, 1955
Papier, Bleistift Paper, pencil
74 x 101,5 cm
Inv.-Nr. K.I. 15154/178

Aula Tribunale „Manlio Capitolo", Venedig Venice
Planpause nach Zeichnung Carlo Scarpas für die Deckenleuchten,
Rahmenprofile im Originalmaß, mit Materialangaben Blueprint after drawing
of ceiling lamps by Carlo Scarpa, frame profiles in original dimensions,
with material specifications, 1955
Papier, Bleistift, gelber Buntstift Paper, pencil, yellow crayon
45,5 x 57 cm
Inv.-Nr. K.I. 15154/179

Aula Tribunale „Manlio Capitolo", Venedig Venice
Planpause nach signierter Zeichnung Carlo Scarpas mit Querschnitt des
Gerichtstisches, in Originalgröße, mit Materialangaben, doppelseitig Blueprint
after signed drawing by Carlo Scarpa with cross-section of judges' table,
original dimensions, with material specifications, recto and verso, 1955
Papier, Bleistift, roter Buntstift, Kugelschreiber Paper, pencil, red crayon,
ballpoint
88 x 75 cm
Inv.-Nr. K.I. 15154/180

Aula Tribunale „Manlio Capitolo", Venedig Venice
Planpause nach signierter Zeichnung Carlo Scarpas mit Seitenansicht der
Sessel in Originalgröße und Aufsicht und Seitenansicht im Maßstab 1:10,
mit Materialangaben Blueprint after signed drawing by Carlo Scarpa with side
view of the chairs in their original dimensions and top view and side view of
the chairs on a scale of 1:10, with material specifications, 1955
Papier, Bleistift, roter Buntstift Paper, pencil, red crayon
129,6 x 74,5 cm
Inv.-Nr. K.I. 15154/181

Aula Tribunale „Manlio Capitolo", Venedig Venice
Planpause nach signierter Zeichnung Carlo Scarpas mit Aufsicht der
Einrichtung im Maßstab 1:25 Blueprint after signed drawing by Carlo Scarpa
with top view of furniture on a scale of 1:25, 1956
Papier, Bleistift, roter Buntstift Paper, pencil, red crayon
29,5 x 73,5 cm
Inv.-Nr. K.I. 15154/182

Aula Tribunale „Manlio Capitolo", Venedig Venice
Planpause nach signierter Zeichnung Carlo Scarpas mit Querschnitt der
Profile der Paneele der Einrichtung im Originalmaßstab, doppelseitig Blueprint
after signed drawing by Carlo Scarpas with cross-section of panel profiles on
their original scale, recto and verso, 1955
Papier, Bleistift, roter Buntstift Paper, pencil, red crayon
41 x 99 cm
Inv.-Nr. K.I. 15154/183

Aula Tribunale „Manlio Capitolo", Venedig Venice
Planpause nach signierter Zeichnung Carlo Scarpas mit Aufriss der
Fensterwand der Einrichtung mit Maßangaben, im Maßstab 1:10, doppelseitig
Blueprint after signed drawing by Carlo Scarpa with elevation of wall with
windows, with measurements, scale 1:10, recto and verso, 1955
Papier, Bleistift, gelber Buntstift Paper, pencil, yellow crayon
48,5 x 102,2 cm
Inv.-Nr. K.I. 15154/184

Aula Tribunale „Manlio Capitolo", Venedig Venice
Planpause nach signierter Zeichnung Carlo Scarpas der Beschläge und Öff-
ner der Fenster im Originalmaß Blueprint after signed drawing of window fittings and openers in their original dimensions by Carlo Scarpa, 1955
Papier, Bleistift, gelber Buntstift Paper, pencil, yellow crayon
89 x 40,5 cm
Inv.-Nr. K.I. 15154/185

Aula Tribunale „Manlio Capitolo", Venedig Venice
Planpause nach signierter Zeichnung Carlo Scarpas mit Aufriss und Querschnitt der Paneele an der Rückseite der Aula Tribunale, mit Maßangaben, Maßstab 1:10, doppelseitig Blueprint after signed drawing by Carlo Scarpa with elevation and cross-section of panels in the rear of the space, with measurements, scale 1:10, recto and verso, 1955
Papier, Bleistift, Kugelschreiber Paper, pencil, ballpoint
48,5 x 75,5 cm
Inv.-Nr. K.I. 15154/186

Aula Tribunale „Manlio Capitolo", Venedig Venice
Planpause nach signierter Zeichnung Carlo Scarpas mit Aufriss und Querschnitt der Paneele an der rechten Seite der Aula Tribunale, mit Maßangaben, Maßstab 1:10, doppelseitig Blueprint after signed drawing by Carlo Scarpa with elevation and cross-section of right-side panels, with measurements, scale 1:10, recto and verso, 1955
Papier, Bleistift, Kugelschreiber Paper, pencil, ballpoint
49,5 x 103 cm
Inv.-Nr. K.I. 15154/187

Aula Tribunale „Manlio Capitolo", Venedig Venice
Planpause nach signierter Zeichnung Carlo Scarpas mit Aufriss und Querschnitt der Paneele der Fensterwand mit Maßangaben, Maßstab 1:10, doppelseitig Blueprint after signed drawing by Carlo Scarpa with elevation and cross-section of panels of wall with windows, with measurements, scale 1:10, recto and verso, 1955
Papier, Bleistift, roter Buntstift Paper, pencil, red crayon
49,5 x 102,5 cm
Inv.-Nr. K.I. 15154/188

Aula Tribunale „Manlio Capitolo", Venedig Venice
Signierte Originalzeichnung Carlo Scarpas für Profile der Einfassungen der Fenster im Originalmaß und im verkleinerten Schema Signed original drawing of window frame profiles in their original dimensions and on a smaller scale by Carlo Scarpa, 1955
Velin, Bleistift Vellum paper, pencil
59,5 x 130 cm
Inv.-Nr. K.I. 15154/189

Aula Tribunale „Manlio Capitolo", Venedig Venice
Skizze Carlo Scarpas für den Tisch der Anwälte, mit Rechnungen Sketch of table for attorneys by Carlo Scarpa, with calculations, 1955
Papier, Bleistift, Kugelschreiber Paper, pencil, ballpoint
23 x 29 cm
Inv.-Nr. K.I. 15154/190

Aula Tribunale „Manlio Capitolo", Venedig Venice
Konstruktionsskizze Carlo Scarpas mit Details für den Tisch der Richter, doppelseitig Construction sketch by Carlo Scarpa with details of the judges' table, recto and verso, 1955
Papier, Bleistift Paper, pencil
22,6 x 29 cm
Inv.-Nr. K.I. 15154/191*   Seite Page 27

Aula Tribunale „Manlio Capitolo", Venedig Venice
Zeichnung Carlo Scarpas mit Grundriss der Aula Tribunale, mit Maßangaben, doppelseitig Drawing by Carlo Scarpa with ground plan, with measurements, recto and verso, 1955
Papier, Bleistift Paper, pencil
18,1 x 24 cm
Inv.-Nr. K.I. 15154/192

Museo di Castelvecchio, Verona
Originalzeichnung Carlo Scarpas, Aufriss, Querschnitte, Aufsicht der Ladenelemente, farbig angelegt, Details, Maßstab 1:10 Original drawing by Carlo Scarpa, elevation, cross-sections, top view of drawers, colored, with details, scale 1:10, 1956–64
Dünner Karton, geklebt, Bleistift, roter, gelber, blauer Buntstift Thin cardboard, repaired with glue, pencil, red, yellow, blue crayon
43,1 x 63,1 cm
Inv.-Nr. K.I. 15154/193*

Tomba Brion, San Vito d'Altivole
Entwurf für die Schiebetür aus Beton, farbig gefasst, Aufriss mit hinzugefügten Detailskizzen Carlo Scarpas zu den Griffen und den Beschlägen und Führungen, mit Maßangaben und Notizen Scarpas Design of concrete sliding door, elevation with added sketches of details concerning the handles, fittings and guides by Carlo Scarpa, with measurements and notes by the architect, 1970–78
Planpause auf Papier, Bleistift, mit rosa, gelbem, orange, blauem, grünem Buntstift gehöht Blueprint on paper, pencil, heightened with pink, yellow, orange, blue, green crayon
Je Each 43,3 x 79,5 cm
Inv.-Nr. K.I. 15154/194, 15154/195*   Seite Page 73

Tomba Brion, San Vito d'Altivole
Decke der Kapelle, Skizze aus dem Atelier Carlo Scarpas, mit Maßangaben und Darstellung der Struktur Ceiling of chapel, sketch by a member of Carlo Scarpa's studio, with measurements and representation of structure, 1970–78
Karton, Bleistift, orange Buntstift Cardboard, pencil, orange crayon
23 x 35 cm
Inv.-Nr. K.I. 15154/196*   Seite Page 78 oben top

Palazzo Querini Stampalia, Venedig Venice
Detailskizze für die Eingangstür, Profile der Konstruktion, Querschnitte, teilweise im Originalmaß, sonst mit Maß- und Materialangaben Sketch with details of entrance door, profiles of construction, cross-section, either in their original dimensions or with measurements and material specifications, 1961–63
Plankopie mit Zeichnung Carlo Scarpas, doppelseitig, Bleistift, orange, gelber Buntstift, Kugelschreiber Blueprint with drawing by Carlo Scarpa, recto and verso, pencil, orange and yellow crayon, ballpoint
53 x 68 cm
Inv.-Nr. K.I. 15154/197*   Seite Page 50

Palazzo Querini Stampalia, Venedig Venice
Zeichnung Carlo Scarpas für eine Vitrine, Anlage des Rahmens und Querschnitt mit Anlage des Kippmechanismus zum Öffnen der Scheibe, Maßstab 1:10 Drawing for a showcase by Carlo Scarpa, structure of frame and cross-section with tilting mechanism for opening of pane, scale 1:10, 1969–63
Velin, Bleistift, roter, blauer Buntstift Vellum paper, pencil, red, blue crayon
32,5 x 101,5 cm
Inv.-Nr. K.I. 15154/198

Ausstellung Exhibition „Venezia e Bisanzio", Palazzo Ducale, Venedig Venice
Zeichnung Carlo Scarpas für die Eingangsgestaltung am oberen Treppenabsatz des Palazzo Ducale, Aufriss mit Maßangaben Drawing by Carlo Scarpa for design of entrance on the upper landing of the palace, elevation with measurements, 1974
Papier, Bleistift, Kugelschreiber, grüner Buntstift Paper, pencil, ballpoint, green crayon
31 x 42 cm
Inv.-Nr. K.I. 15154/199

Olivetti-Schauraum, Venedig Olivetti showroom, Venice
Perspektive und Aufsicht der Treppe mit Anlage der Abfolge der Stufen Perspective and top view of staircase with sequence of stairs, 1957/58
Velin, Bleistift Vellum paper, pencil
30 x 44,5 cm
Inv.-Nr. K.I. 15154/200*   Seite Page 35

Waffenmuseum Museum of Ancient Weapons**, Castello di Brescia, Brescia**
4 Entwurfszeichnungen, doppelseitig, mit maßgetreuen Details der Stäbe mit Gelenksverbindungen und Bohrlöchern 4 design drawings, recto and verso, with true-to-scale details of the bars, with joints and drill holes, 1971
Entwurfskarton, gestückelt, Bleistift, roter, blauer, gelber Buntstift Cardboard, pieced together, pencil, red, blue, yellow crayon
69,5 x 54 cm
Inv.-Nr. K.I. 15154/201/1–4

Ausstellungsgestaltungen für Venedig, Rom, Mailand Exhibition designs for Venice, Rome, Milan
7 Originalskizzen Carlo Scarpas für Ausstellungsgestaltungen, etwa Sockel und Vitrinen, Maßstab 1:10 7 original sketches by Carlo Scarpa, such as for bases and showcases, scale 1:10, 1949–59
Velin, Schreibpapier, Karton, Bleistift, roter, gelber Buntstift, gelber Filzstift, Kugelschreiber Vellum paper, writing paper, cardboard, pencil, red, yellow crayon, yellow felt tip, ballpoint
15 x 21 cm (1, 2), 23,6 x 20 cm (3), 22 x 28 cm (4), 21 x 31 cm (5, 6), 20,8 x 31 cm (7)
Inv.-Nr. K.I. 15154/202/1–7

Ausstellungsgestaltungen für Venedig, Rom, Mailand Exhibition designs for Venice, Rome, Milan
13 Originalskizzen Carlo Scarpas für Ausstellungsgestaltungen, etwa Biennale Venedig, Sockel, Vitrinen und Wandgestaltungen 13 original sketches by Carlo Scarpa, such as for bases, showcases, and wall designs of the Venice Biennial, 1949–59
Velin, Schreibpapier, Karton, Bleistift, orange, grüner Buntstift, Kugelschreiber Vellum paper, writing paper, cardboard, pencil, orange, green crayon, ballpoint
21 x 31 cm (1), 22 x 28 cm (2), 41,5 x 31 cm (3), 21,5 x 20 cm (4), 5 x 21 cm (5), 21 x 30 cm (6), 21,5 x 28 cm (7), 5 x 21 cm (8), 8,5 x 12 cm (9), 10 x 21 cm (10, 11), 20,5 x 15,5 cm (12), 21 x 15 cm (13)
Inv.-Nr. K.I. 15154/203/1–13

Architekturfakultät der Universität Venedig Department of Architecture, Venice University, Aula Magna di Ca' Foscari
Planpause Carlo Scarpas für die stereometrische Ansicht der Türwand mit Anlage der Fensterfüllungen und Türen Blueprint by Carlo Scarpa of the stereometric view of the Aula door wall with window sashes and doors, 1955/56
Bleistift Pencil
59,5 x 206 cm
Inv.-Nr. K.I. 15154/204/1   Seite Page 33

Architekturfakultät der Universität Venedig Department of Architecture, Venice University, Aula Magna di Ca' Foscari
Planpause Carlo Scarpas für den Grundriss im Maßstab 1:50 Blueprint by Carlo Scarpa of the ground plan, scale 1:50, 1955/56
Bleistift Pencil
59,5 x 62,3 cm
Inv.-Nr. K.I. 15154/204/2

Architekturfakultät der Universität Venedig Department of Architecture, Venice University, Aula Magna di Ca' Foscari
Planpause Carlo Scarpas für die Ansicht der Türwand mit Anlage der Fensterfüllungen und Türen Blueprint by Carlo Scarpa of Aula door wall with window sashes and doors, 1955/56
59,5 x 61 cm
Inv.-Nr. K.I. 15154/204/3

Architekturfakultät der Universität Venedig Department of Architecture, Venice University, Aula Magna di Ca' Foscari
Planpause Carlo Scarpas für die Ansicht der Türwand mit Anlage der Fensterfüllungen und Türen Blueprint by Carlo Scarpa of Aula door wall with window sashes and doors, 1955/56
59,5 x 84 cm
Inv.-Nr. K.I. 15154/204/4*

Architekturfakultät der Universität Venedig Department of Architecture, Venice University, Aula Magna di Ca' Foscari
Planpause Carlo Scarpas für die Wandpaneele der Türwand mit Maßangaben Blueprint by Carlo Scarpa of the wall panels of the Aula door wall, with measurements, 1955/56
55,2 x 120 cm
Inv.-Nr. K.I. 15154/204/5

Architekturfakultät der Universität Venedig Department of Architecture, Venice University, Aula Magna di Ca' Foscari
Planpause Carlo Scarpas für ein Grundrissdetail der Türseite mit Maßangaben, Aufsicht Blueprint by Carlo Scarpa of ground plan detail of the Aula door side, with measurements, top view, 1955/56
Bleistift Pencil
55,6 x 31 cm
Inv.-Nr. K.I. 15154/204/6

Architekturfakultät der Universität Venedig Department of Architecture, Venice University, Aula Magna di Ca' Foscari
Planpause Carlo Scarpas für ein Grundrissdetail der Türseite mit Maßangaben, Aufsicht Blueprint by Carlo Scarpa of ground plan detail of the Aula door side, with measurements, top view, 1955/56
Bleistift Pencil
58 x 71 cm
Inv.-Nr. K.I. 15154/204/7

Architekturfakultät der Universität Venedig Department of Architecture, Venice University, Aula Magna di Ca' Foscari
Planpause Carlo Scarpas für ein Grundrissdetail der Türseite mit Maßangaben, Aufsicht Blueprint by Carlo Scarpa of ground plan detail of the Aula door side, with measurements, top view, 1955/56
Bleistift Pencil
46 x 31,5 cm
Inv.-Nr. K.I. 15154/204/8

Architekturfakultät der Universität Venedig Department of Architecture, Venice University, Aula Magna di Ca' Foscari
Planpause Carlo Scarpas für ein Grundrissdetail der Türseite mit Maßangaben, Aufsicht Blueprint by Carlo Scarpa of ground plan detail of the Aula door side, with measurements, top view, 1955/56
Bleistift Pencil
43,6 x 45 cm
Inv.-Nr. K.I. 15154/204/9

Architekturfakultät der Universität Venedig Department of Architecture, Venice University, Aula Magna di Ca' Foscari
Planpause Carlo Scarpas für die Wandpaneele der Türwand mit Maßangaben Blueprint by Carlo Scarpa of the wall panels of the Aula door wall, with measurements, 1955/56
Bleistift Pencil
56 x 91,5 cm
Inv.-Nr. K.I. 15154/204/10

Architekturfakultät der Universität Venedig Department of Architecture, Venice University, Aula Magna di Ca' Foscari
Planpause Carlo Scarpas für die Wandpaneele der Türwand mit Maß- und Materialangaben Blueprint by Carlo Scarpa of the wall panels of the Aula door wall, with measurements and material specifications, 1955/56
Bleistift Pencil
58,2 x 92 cm
Inv.-Nr. K.I. 15154/204/11

Architekturfakultät der Universität Venedig Department of Architecture, Venice University, Aula Magna di Ca' Foscari
Planpause Carlo Scarpas für die Wandpaneele der Türwand, Details der Profile, Maßstab 1:10 Blueprint by Carlo Scarpa of the wall panels of the Aula door wall, details of profiles, scale 1:10, 1955/56
Bleistift Pencil
59 x 91,5 cm
Inv.-Nr. K.I. 15154/204/12

Architekturfakultät der Universität Venedig Department of Architecture, Venice University, Aula Magna di Ca' Foscari
Ausstellungsinstallation, Originalskizze, Details für Pfosten in Nut- und Feder-Verbindung, handschriftliche Vermerke Exhibition installation, original sketch, details for posts with tongue and groove connections, handwritten comments 1955/56
Velin, Bleistift Vellum paper, pencil
35 x 37,5 cm
Inv.-Nr. K.I. 15154/205/1

2 Entwürfe für einen Schrank in Formica 2 designs for a Formica cupboard
Aufriss und Detail der Profile Elevation and profile details
Papier, Bleistift Paper, pencil
21 x 27,5 cm (2), 22 x 28 cm (3)
Inv.-Nr. K.I. 15154/205/2, 3

Entwürfe für einen Schrank in Formica Designs for a Formica cupboard
Planpause nach Skizze für einen Schrank, Aufriss und Rahmen Blueprint after sketch, elevation and frame
Papier, Bleistift, Kugelschreiber Paper, pencil, ballpoint
58,5 x 58 cm
Inv.-Nr. K.I. 15154/206

Modelle Models

Haus Zentner, Zürich Zentner House, Zurich
Aufbau der Tischplatte des Speisezimmers Structure of dining room table top, 1967/68
Schichtverleimtes Makassar-Ebenholz, Marmor, Mahagoni Plywood (Makassar ebony), mahogany, marble
44 x 33 x 8 cm
Inv.-Nr. K.I. 15154/207*

Olivetti-Schauraum, Venedig Olivetti showroom, Venice
Metallgitter Metal grille, 1957/58
Ramin
24,2 x 20,5 x 2,5 cm
Inv.-Nr. K.I. 15154/208*

Tomba Brion San Vito d'Altivole
Inschrift im Sarkophagdeckel Inscription for sarcophagus lid, 1970–78
Makassar-Ebenholz, Einsatzstücke aus Elfenbein Makassar ebony with ivory inlays
7,7 x 69,5 x 2,5 cm
Inv.-Nr. K.I. 15154/209*   Seite Page 87 unten bottom

Tomba Brion, San Vito d'Altivole
Holzpaneele, Holz, mit Einsatzstücken aus Metall, mit Profilschnitten und Fräsungen Wood panels, with metal inlays, vertical sections and shapings, 1970–78
Makassar-Ebenholz (1, 2), Metall, Fichtenholz (3) Makassar ebony (1, 2), metal, deal (3)
15 x 74,5 x 4,5 cm (1); 69,5 x 7,9 x 3 cm (2); 37,5 x 12,6 x 1 cm (3)
Inv.-Nr. K.I. 15154/210/1, 2, 3*   Seite Page 89

Tomba Brion, San Vito d'Altivole
Stäbe des Leuchters, Holz, mit Einsatzstücken aus anderen Hölzern, gedrechselt Bars of chandeliers, wood with other woods inlaid, turned, 1970–78
Rio-Palisander (1), Makassar-Ebenholz (2), Teak, Ebenholz (3), Birne, Ebenholz (4), Rio rosewood (1), Makassar ebony (2), teak, ebony (3), pear, ebony (4)
15 x 3 cm (1); 8 x 5 cm (2); 4 x 2 cm (3); 8 x 2 cm (4)
Inv.-Nr. K.I. 15154/211/1–4*   Seite Page 89

Waffenmuseum Museum of Ancient Weapons Castello di Brescia, Brescia
Transennen des Treppengeländers Transennae of banister, 1971
Ramin
16,1 x 16,1 cm (1); 12,6 x 12,6 cm (2)
Inv.-Nr. K.I. 15154/212/1, 2*   Seite Page 89

Tomba Brion, San Vito d'Altivole
Kassette zum Kruzifix Crucifix box, 1970–78
Weichholz, Fichte Softwood, deal
65,5 x 42 x 9,5 cm (geschlossen closed)
Inv.-Nr. K.I. 15154/213*   Seite Page 88 unten bottom

Tomba Brion, San Vito d'Altivole
Ecklösung der Umfassungsmauer Corner solution of walling, 1970–78
Ramin
13 x 13 x 16 cm
Inv.-Nr. K.I. 15154/214*   Seite Page 86

Palazzo Querini Stampalia
Handlauf der Zugangsbrücke und der Haupttreppe im Gebäude Access bridge and main staircase handrails, 1961–63
Ebenholz, geschnitten (1), Ramin (2) Ebony, cut (1), Ramin (2)
Inv.-Nr. K.I. 15154/215   Seite Page 89

* Gezeigt in der MAK-Ausstellung „Carlo Scarpa. Das Handwerk der Architektur"
* As shown in the MAK Exhibition "Carlo Scarpa. The Craft of Architecture"

Ausstellung „Carlo Scarpa. Die andere Stadt"
Exhibition "Carlo Scarpa. The Other City"
MAK-Ausstellungshalle Exhibition Hall, 1989/90

Rekonstruktion der Installation „La Poesia",
errichtet im Rahmen der Expo Montreal 1967
Reconstruction of the installation "La Poesia",
erected in the course of the Expo Montreal 1967

MAK WIEN VIENNA

C.E.O. and Artistic Director
Peter Noever

SUPERVISORY BOARD
Andreas Treichl Vorsitzender Chairman (C.E.O. Erste Bank, Wien Vienna)
Rudolf Scholten Stellvertretender Vorsitzender (Mitglied des Vorstands der Österreichischen Kontrollbank) Vice-Chairman (Board of Directors, Österreichische Kontrollbank)
Ingrid Gazzari C.E.O. WIIW, Wien Vienna
Roman Koller Landesschulrat für die Steiermark Styrian Schoolboard
Georg Mayer MAK
Wolfgang Polzhuber Bundesministerium für Wirtschaft und Arbeit Federal Ministry of Economic Affairs
August Ruhs Universität Wien University of Vienna
Gottfried Toman Finanzprokuratur Office of State Attorneys
Silvia Zendron Bundesministerium für Finanzen Federal Ministry of Finance

MAK CENTER FOR ART AND ARCHITECTURE, LOS ANGELES

Schindler House
835 North Kings Road
West Hollywood, CA 90069, USA
Tel. (+1-323) 651 1510
Fax (+1-323) 651 2340
E-Mail: office@MAKcenter.org
www.MAKcenter.org

MAK GOVERNING COMMITTEE
Brigitte Böck
Harriett F. Gold
Peter Noever
Barbara Redl
Joseph Secky
Robert L. Sweeney
Peter Launsky-Tieffenthal Advisory Member

DIRECTOR
Kimberli Meyer

CAT GROUP

Zur Förderung der Entwicklung und Realisierung des CAT Established to promote the development and realization of CAT – Contemporary Art Tower
Johannes Strohmayer Präsident President
Karl Newole Vizepräsident Vice-President

CAT INTERNATIONAL ADVISORY BOARD
Catherine David
Boris Groys
Cornelius Grupp
Andreas Treichl
Paul Virilio

MAK ART SOCIETY WIEN VIENNA

Zur Förderung des MAK Established to promote and support the MAK
Stubenring 5, A-1010 Wien Vienna, Austria
Tel. (+43-1) 711 36-207, Fax (+43-1) 711 36-213
E-Mail: MAKartsociety@MAK.at

VORSTAND BOARD OF DIRECTORS
Ingrid Gazzari Präsidentin President
Peter Noever Stellvertretender Präsident Vice-President
Gregor Eichinger Schriftführer Keeper of the Minutes
Manfred Wakolbinger Kassier Cashier
Cornelius Grupp
Michael Hochenegg
Wolfgang M. Rosam
Eva Schlegel

EXECUTIVE OFFICE
Michaela Hartig

Johannes Strohmayer Rechnungsprüfer Auditor
Arno Hirschvogl Rechnungsprüfer Auditor

MAK ARTIST BOARD
Vito Acconci, New York
Coop Himmelb(l)au, Wien Vienna
Bruno Gironcoli, Wien Vienna
Zaha M. Hadid, London
Jenny Holzer, New York
Dennis Hopper, Los Angeles
Rebecca Horn, Bad König
Magdalena Jetelová, Bergheim Thorr
Ilya & Emilia Kabakov, New York
Jannis Kounellis, Rom Rome
Maria Lassnig, Wien Vienna
Thom Mayne, Los Angeles
Oswald Oberhuber, Wien Vienna
Roland Rainer, Wien Vienna
Kiki Smith, New York
Franz West, Wien Vienna
Lebbeus Woods, New York
Heimo Zobernig, Wien Vienna

INTERNATIONAL MAK ADVISORY BOARD
Gerti Gürtler, Präsidentin President, Wien Vienna
James Dyson, London
Rolf Fehlbaum, Basel
Ernfried Fuchs, Wien Vienna
Francesca von Habsburg, Salzburg
Heinz F. Hofer-Wittmann, Etsdorf/Kamp
Eva-Maria von Höfer, Wien Vienna
Ursula Kwizda, Wien Vienna
Ronald S. Lauder, New York
Franz-Hesso zu Leiningen, Tegernsee
Alexander Mayr, Wien Vienna
Veronika Piech, Wien Vienna
Thaddaeus Ropac, Salzburg
Frederick & Laurie Samitaur Smith, Los Angeles
W. Michael Satke, Wien Vienna
Penelope Seidler, Sydney
Jorge Vergara, Zapopan
Iwan Wirth, Zürich Zurich